THE MASTERS ON THE DRY FLY

Also edited by J. MICHAEL MIGEL

The Stream Conservation Handbook

THE MASTERS ON THE DRY FLY

Edited by **J. Michael Migel**

Illustrated by **Dave Whitlock**

J. B. Lippincott Company

Philadelphia and New York

U.S. Library of Congress Cataloging in Publication Data

Main entry under title:

The Masters on the dry fly.

    1. Fly fishing.   I. Migel, J. Michael.
SH456.M32   799.1′2   77-2656
ISBN-0-397-01188-1

Contents

CONTENTS

Foreword

Nick Lyons

THE PAST TWENTY YEARS have been remarkable ones for fly fishermen. During that time major organizations such as the Federation of Fly Fishermen and Trout Unlimited have been founded and vastly expanded, literally hundreds of books on the subject have appeared, there has been a proliferation of new tackle, a bewildering array of sophisticated fly patterns have been introduced, and a new magazine, *Fly Fisherman*, has emerged, whose circulation has soared from under 20,000 to nearly 100,000. If for a while after World War II there was some doubt as to whether fly fishing could withstand the onslaught of spinning, today there is no doubt whatsoever. Fly fishing is very much alive and well. If there is any problem, it is that so much new information and equipment and so many new fly patterns, theories, and techniques have caused confusion. The time has come for consolidation and distillation.

Fishing the dry fly, often considered the epitome of fly fishing, is a good place to start, though, as Roderick Haig-Brown wisely notes, "There are times when a dry fly is poor technique, an affectation rather than an honest conviction."

What is the allure or "charm" of dry-fly fishing?

What are its traditions, where is it headed?

What tackle and techniques are available to modern anglers—and which are best?

What are the basic dry-fly waters and how should we best fish them?

What fish will we seek with the dry fly—and how?

Where shall we fish?

Mike Migel, who conceived and developed this book, was clearly aware of these questions. He wanted a book that would bring together the best that is thought and practiced on the subject (and in the future he foresees a substantial number of other books in this series, similarly conceived, on many other aspects of fishing).

There are individual author-fishermen who might have written the whole of such a book as *The Masters on the Dry Fly*. But precisely where this becomes a compendium of different fly fishermen writing about their specialty, it differs from that kind of book and reveals its unique value. It is a coordinated treasury. It captures both the romance and the mechanics of perhaps the most pleasurable form of fly fishing. There are anglers who fish only with dry flies and consider it the highest form of fly fishing; this book is not necessarily for them but for anyone who ever uses any kind of dry fly—beginner, intermediate, or expert— or for someone who would like to start. It is for anyone who takes pleasure in that sweet electric shock of watching a good fish rise.

In chapters specially written for this book, sixteen of the finest angling authors of our time have shared dreams, theories, trips, and skills related to dry-fly fishing. Roderick L. Haig-Brown, in one of the last pieces he wrote before his recent and untimely death, speaks movingly about the incomparable charm of the dry fly. He is perhaps the one author I would call indispensable for the literate angler, the one angling author through whom the mainstream of fly-fishing culture runs most clearly; we shall miss him and are fortunate indeed to have his contribution to this book. Next, "Pal" Alexander and Ed Zern bring us up to date on the history of the dry fly in Europe and America. Poul Jorgensen, the superb flytier and instructor, gives us practical information on the dry fly itself, and Charlie Waterman explores the dry-fly man's best tackle. Helpful casting advice and special presentations are offered by Lefty Kreh, Charles Fox, and Ernie Schwiebert, while Steve Raymond, Michael Fong, Dave Whitlock, and Lee Wulff offer exceptional chapters on fishing still water and big water for such varied game as bass, panfish, and Atlantic salmon. There's a fine short piece by Art Flick on the too-little-recognized importance and technique of pocket-water fishing, and a long chapter, drawn from his broad experience, by that master, Len Wright. Carl Richards, here operating solo, supplies a helpful treatment of basic entomology a dry-fly fisherman should know, and Bob Warner lets us share some of the exotic and rare delights of the peripatetic angler.

What a superb feast! Sweet and useful. It offers diversity and breadth, more than a bit of poetry combined with the hard specifics of how-to, something for the angler who fishes the East or West—or abroad.

Of course, a few good ones got away. There are some other authors I'd have liked to have seen in this book: some, I understand, could not meet a tight deadline, one (in unfounded modesty) refused, several had other commitments. Most of these will contribute to subsequent volumes in this important series.

Mike Migel, who tried to save our waters in his highly acclaimed *Stream Conservation Handbook*, here helps us know some good things to do with them if, in time, they're still there. That's a major consideration—and one that provides the somber but challenging final note to this book.

Ever since I was a child and watched a large native brook trout rise in an unnamed Catskill creek, its awesome symmetry engraved forever on my brain, I have loved the idea of fishing the surface for game fish. Nothing in angling compares to the sight of a fish taking a surface offering. *The Masters on the Dry Fly* captures that excitement and will add to your pleasure and success; it has to mine.

THE
MASTERS
ON THE
DRY FLY

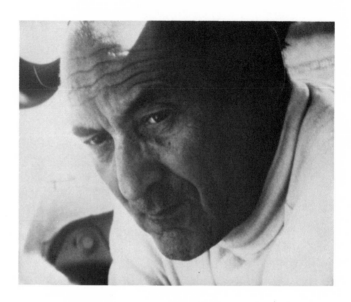

Roderick Haig-Brown was born in England in 1908 but lived most of his adult life on Vancouver Island, along the banks of the Campbell River, a river that provided a never-ending source of material for his many articles and books.

In 1973 he completed a term as chancellor of the University of Victoria, and in 1975 he finished his service as a judge of the Provincial Court of British Columbia.

His death in the late summer of 1976 was a tremendous loss to the forces of conservation and to the many, many thousands of fishermen who had enjoyed and learned much from such classics of nature and angling writing as A River Never Sleeps, Fisherman's Winter, Fisherman's Spring, Fisherman's Summer, and Fisherman's Fall; and from articles in Canadian literature and such U.S. magazines as The New Yorker, Atlantic Monthly, and Sports Illustrated.

His contributions to conservation were great. He was a director of the National Second Century Fund, a trustee of the Nature Conservancy of Canada, adviser to the British Columbia Wildlife Federation, Senior Adviser to Trout Unlimited (U.S.) and to the Federation of Fly Fishermen (U.S.), and Honorary Director of Theodore Gordon Flyfishers (New York). In 1970 he was appointed to the International Pacific Salmon Fisheries Commission, and his book The Salmon was made part of Canada's presentation at The Law of the Sea Conference in 1974.

1. Charm of the Dry Fly

Roderick Haig-Brown

THE ESSENTIAL CHARM of dry-fly fishing is in the certainty of seeing the fish in natural response to the fly before it is hooked. Under many conditions it is possible to see the fish long before one even casts for it and, with big fish, through the whole long, slow movement of the rise itself. Sometimes one sees only the rise itself and just the intimation of the fish under it; sometimes one sees nothing more than the fragment of a glimpse as the floating artificial disappears in the tiny dimple of the rise. But one has seen it and has seen the fly go down, so the response is to something visible above the surface, not just to the feel of an underwater pull. True, the take is often seen in nymphing, especially upstream nymphing, or in fishing a wet fly just under the surface film. But in dry-fly fishing it is *always* seen, unless the fisherman's attention is attracted elsewhere at just the wrong moment, as has been known to happen.

The classic dry-fly streams are the chalk streams of Britain and northern France, the limestone streams of the eastern United States, and the spring creeks of the Rockies and elsewhere. The classic dry-fly fish is certainly the brown trout because of its habit of holding on station just under the surface and gently intercepting drifting insects, often selecting with care one species out of several that may be hatching. The brown trout is impressive, too, under these conditions because it is likely to be sophisticated if it is of any size and extremely sensitive to the slightest drag of the leader on the drifting fly.

The situation of a brown trout rising steadily in some awkward spot in a brilliantly clear stream is probably the ultimate test of the fly fisher's skills. If the fish is to be risen and securely hooked, the deception must be total. The fly must be placed precisely from an angle and a distance that conceal the fisherman and his movements. The fly must be the right one or some deliberately chosen variation from it. The float must be perfect, a drift with the current as natural as though the fly were unattached. The fish must rise and take the fly in complete faith. The fisherman's response must be exactly timed, firm enough to set the hook, and smooth enough to avoid any risk of breaking the leader.

This is elegant performance on the part of both fish and fisherman, and the dry-fly purists of my youthful memories were inclined to be arrogant about it. I was raised on a chalk stream and developed a full measure of arrogance, even though I was not a purist. I felt a little uneasy about nymph fishing, but I enjoyed it and did very well with Skues's techniques. Knowing little or nothing of it, I call wet-fly fishing "chuck and chance it." To have a good fish rise and become securely hooked on an obviously dragging fly was a matter for shame, not satisfaction. It was sinful.

All the arrogance and soul-searching really reflected the fact that drag is the true bane of the dry-fly fisherman. We even recognized what we called "invisible drag," because the wise old brown trout certainly recognized it in some of their holding spots and either ignored the fly or quickly sank from sight and went off the feed. With the wet fly drag did not matter and with the nymph it mattered far less, though I usually tried hard to avoid it.

Lure of the dry fly.

Hairwing dry fly.

One grows older, horizons grow wider, tolerance grows greater. There is the realization, well known to good fly fishermen since Charles Cotton and probably long before, that there is bottom and middle to the water as well as top. There are trout other than brown trout, streams other than chalk streams, aquatic forage other than the delicate mayfly duns and the unreliable evening sedges of the chalk streams. Controlling a wet fly, holding it, drifting it, working it becomes high art, as difficult and sensitive as the art of the dry fly. The streams are big and rough, the fish are no longer visible; one must read the water, sense where the fish are, search intelligently, and still with skillful hands to find them.

Yet the attraction of the dry fly remains. The perfect deception and the visible rise to the fly seen on the surface of the water are still joys and excitements to be experienced and loved again. One searches in the light of new understanding.

I first saw the hairwing fly over rough water on the McKenzie River in Oregon nearly fifty years ago. It shocked me to see it fished downstream, across the stream, with two flies on the leader or even three. There was no particular concern about drag, very little about the fly drawing under. The fish loved it, though it seemed to me that half a dozen were missed for every one properly hooked, and all of them should have been scared out of their wits.

Except perhaps in the spring creeks, rainbow and cutthroat trout in the West do not often hold in one place and calmly accept what the run of the river brings them. Even brown trout move more and are less certain to be found in one obvious feeding place. Usually one must search for them, so the dry fly becomes almost, but not quite, chuck and chance it. I still prefer the upstream cast and the straight drift without drag, and for the most part I know where to place my cast. I now delight in the float of a big hairwing over broken water and the expectation it brings. I can usually move more fish by throwing the fly across, letting it drag, bouncing it upstream, and letting it drop back in a straight drift. I enjoy all these techniques immensely, but I am still just a little ashamed of them. So much of the deceit is in artificial motion that the fly becomes more nearly a lure than a fly.

I do not really think that a dry-fly purist can be called a good fly fisherman: he is certainly not a well-rounded fly fisherman. There are times when a dry fly is a poor technique, an affectation rather than an honest conviction. But there are other times, many other times, when a dry fly, properly fished, will bring more action and excitement than any other method. If anyone had told me when I was young that I should be fishing a floating fly over fish of 10 and even 20 pounds in the full expectation of rising them and hooking them, I should have thought it a wild dream. Yet I do it now, knowing well that I shall get results I would be unlikely to get otherwise.

From time to time on West Coast streams it is possible to come upon a good fly hatch that has big cutthroats holding station like brown trout and taking fly after fly. It is important to recognize the moment, identify the hatch, and fish the closest possible imitation. Several times I have done extremely well with a size 17 or 18 iron blue on such occasions, usually in early spring. In nontidal streams both cutthroats and rainbows often rise well to naturals on the surface, and I have almost always found that a floating fly considerably larger than the naturals works far better than any attempt to exact imitation. This sort of fishing departs very little from the traditional. On Chilean and Argentine streams I learned that big browns and rainbows can be found by floating flies over likely places right in the middle of the day, under the full brightness of the sun. On a northern British Columbia stream I have found rainbows of 4 pounds and over under the same hot, staringly bright midday conditions by their own quiet rises and have been able to move them at once to the honest drift of a small dry fly.

All these could be called difficult uses, calling for technique scarcely less sound and finished than does the brown trout of the chalk stream or the spring creek. For this reason they are both fascinating and exciting. But I think the most exciting application of the floating fly is its use for summer steelhead and Atlantic salmon in low water. In broken water, technique does not matter too much; a clumsy cast, a heavy leader, even a dragging fly may still do all that is needed. But setting the hook can test the fisherman's experience and steadiness; the infinitely slow head and tail roll of a 10- or 15-pound fish, the sudden swift follow-back for fifteen or twenty feet to take the fly that has floated past, the rise that misses the fly altogether and will probably be followed by a second rise that takes it under must all be met by the appropriately deliberate response or lack of response. All are exciting and sometimes breathtaking.

In fast and broken water, steelhead and other trout will come hard at a dragging fly, and, in a sense, a dragging fly may be the easiest way to find them; one can swing it across the current, give it plenty of life and action, and search a lot of water in a short time. But I prefer to try a natural drift first, because the rises to it are much more solid and the fish is much more likely to be properly hooked. In low water, when steelhead are lying motionless on the bottom of a smooth pool, I find I can usually get them moving by repeated casts of a spider on a 3X or 4X leader. Here, too, I use a straight drift at least until the fly passes downstream from me, if only because the shadow of the leader is too much if the fly is skated, and it often takes thirty or forty casts to get two or three fish moving nervously under it. As soon as fish are moving at all, I change to a larger fly and a heavier leader, which almost always produces an immediate rise. But sometimes a fish comes up to the spider before I decide to change, which leaves me a little overmatched except on small streams.

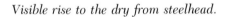

Visible rise to the dry from steelhead.

The visible rise of a fish of 10 or 12 pounds, even 6 or 7 pounds, through several feet of clear water to a surface fly is a very high experience indeed. It is not the same experience as the chalk stream brown trout offers. It is an entirely different order of deception. One is not presenting an exact imitation of an aquatic insect to a confidently feeding fish. Rather, one is working on some built-in reaction of a nonfeeding fish, attempting to trip a remembered response by offering a clumsy terrestrial creature. If the spider has been used first, one has brought the reaction closer to the surface by creating an artificial hatch. The full reward is in the rise itself. Sometimes it is nervous, sudden and splashy, but more often it is a long, slow movement to perfect interception; when that happens it lives in the mind's eye for a long, long time.

I have never fished one of the good eastern Canadian streams with a dry fly for Atlantic salmon, but I have tried in Iceland, with some modest success. The fish are almost always responsive in some way— their fins quiver, they lift a little in the water, they may circle and rise to within an inch of the fly and still not take it. Once in a while a fish will take what one offers, and it seems for a moment that the problem is solved. Unfortunately, the Icelandic fish take a size 8 or 10 fly fished just under the surface film so readily and so consistently that the floating fly seems like an aberration rather than serious fishing, and I, for one, have not given it the trial it probably deserves.

Sometimes I wonder what Frederic M. Halford would have thought of these unorthodox ways of fishing a floating fly. Not much, I imagine, unless some caustic comment had suggested itself, though the chance of a head and tail rise from a 20-pounder might have tempted even him. Theodore Gordon, I am sure, would have had no difficulty or hesitation at all, and it is a pity he never had a chance at Western streams with modern hairwing patterns.

Leaping salmon hooked on hairwing dry.

Mayfly spinner.

I have written nothing of lakes, where a big trout cruising among a heavy hatch can be a great experience. But I wonder how many fly fishermen know that still summer evenings on northern lakes will often yield almost the same experience with cruising lake whitefish up to 4 or 5 pounds? They cruise faithfully and steadily to a line and offer the same challenge as cruising brown trout in the drawn-out suspense of their slow approach.

In the summer of 1971 I revisited some of the English streams where I had learned to fish a dry fly and became almost notoriously successful. I had come from Iceland with stiffish 4-ounce rod and a forward-taper line, and I found myself clumsy and awkward. I did not do well at all, and although my awkwardness was seen only by myself, I found it rather humiliating after a lifetime of fishing to end up less competent than I had been fifty years earlier. Perhaps the only thing I can do now is to go out and restore my confidence by bouncing hairwings around in broken water, while admitting that that hovering brown trout in a quiet meadow stream probably *is* the most difficult of them all.

An hour or so ago I was watching a spent spinner on the smooth surface of a quiet pool. It was flat on the water, wings spread, drifting with the will of the current. But it wasn't quiet. It struggled almost continuously, trying to lift its wings from the water and sending out a succession of soft concentric ripples that leveled off an inch or so away from its body. How does a fisherman achieve exact imitation of that? Perhaps this is one of the reasons why a wise old trout is so seldom fooled by what seems a perfect float.

My Favorite Places to Fish	*Type of Fish*	*Best Time*	*Suggested Flies* Type	*Size*
Campbell River, British Columbia	Steelhead Cutthroat	July– September	1. Steelhead Bee 2. Orange Caddis 3. Humpy	6–10 8–10 8–10
Stellaco River, British Columbia	Rainbow	July– August	1. Candy Fly 2. Yellow Caddis 3. Ginger Spider	10 10 14
Collon Cura, Argentina	Brown Rainbow	February– March	1. Purple Upright 2. Humpy 3. Orange Caddis	10 10 8
Odele Creek, Montana	Brown	Early fall	1. Royal Wulff 2. Iron Blue 3. Adams	16 18 16
Any small West Coast stream with a good summer run	Steelhead	June– September	1. Steelhead Bee 2. Ginger Spider	6–10 14

A. I. *"Pal" Alexander lived in Andover, Massachusetts, where he was the chief executive of Alexander Industries, a cordage company.*

He was a former director of the Federation of Fly Fishermen, United Fly Tyers, Inc., and the Andover Fly Fishers. He was the recipient of the FFF President's Award and the Wayne Buszek Memorial Award for fly-tying.

He also served as a trustee of the Museum of American Fly Fishing in Manchester, Vermont, and conservation commissioner in the town of Andover.

As a writer, he worked as a free-lance journalist and was the outdoor columnist for the Lawrence Eagle Tribune. *His untimely death in December 1976 must surely grieve the entire angling fraternity.*

2. The Beginnings
Exploring Dry-fly Origins

A. I. "Pal" Alexander

THE DRY FLY certainly isn't the most difficult method of fishing, although at times it may be the most productive. For many, perhaps most, fly fishermen it is *the* way to fish for trout. The size of the fish is less important than whether the fly and presentation are correct. Success means a "take" and the playing, landing, and size of the fish are secondary; of course, if it is a large fish, so much the better. Who invented this marvelous thing—the dry fly?

The first reference of merit approaching a floating fly occurs in a *Booke of Fishing* (1590) by Leonard Mascall, who pirated the dressings of Dame Juliana's "Jury" of twelve flies in *The Treatise of Fishing with an Angle* (1496). After giving the dressing of his dark or drake fly, Mascall says, "Thus are they made upon the hooke, lapt about with some corke like each Fly afore mentioned."

The cork obviously helped to ride the fly higher in the water, but by no stretch of the imagination could it be considered a dry fly. Thomas Barker, in *Barker's Delight* (1657), refers to the wool of a red heifer in making a good body, "for I finde it floateth best and procurest the best sport." Like Mascall, Barker, a top-notch pre-Walton fisherman, found a fly on or near the surface readily taken, but, again, we cannot accept this as the dry fly as we know it.

William Shipley, in *A True Treatise on the Art of Fly Fishing* (1838), comes close to our understanding of dry-fly fishing when he says:

> Let your flies float gently down the water, working them gradually towards you, and making a fresh cast every two or three yards you fish. We distinctly recommend frequent casting. A fish gener-

ally takes the fly immediately [after] it has touched the water—provided always it be delicately and lightly flung—and the quick repetition of casting whisks the water out of your flies and line, and consequently keeps them drier and lighter than if they were left to float a longer time in the water.

Shipley, too, realized the angling benefits of floating his cast of wet flies on the surface.

John Waller Hills, the eminent angling historian, in *A History of Fly Fishing for Trout* (1921), mentions Robert Boyle, *Occasional Reflections Upon Several Subjects* (1665), James Wallwork, *The Modern Angler* (1847), and George Scotcher, in his rare *The Fly Fisher's Legacy* (1800), as all referring to trout taken on the surface but not with a dry fly. They refer to a wet fly taken "dry" on the surface but not a fly tied deliberately to float. Furthermore, Hills stipulates that to be a true dry fly it must be switched back and forth in the air to be dried.

The first mention of the dry fly, as defined by Hills and as we generally know it, emerged full blown in George P. R. Pulman's *Vade Mecum of Fly Fishing for Trout*, in the third edition (1851). There is no argument here; the dry fly is described in full, floating above the fish and switched through the air by false casts to dispel the moisture. Many angling historians have been content to accept this as the beginning, but is it?

James Ogden, in his little volume *Ogden on Fly Tying* (1879), proclaims with typical immodesty, "It is well known that I am the inventor of floating flies, the Seat Basket, and the Spring Folding Landing Net, which is so conveniently carried on the basket strip; also the celebrated Devil Killers, which have proved so deadly that they have been prohibited on many streams." Moreover, Ogden reiterates his claim on the invention of the dry fly several more times in the text and states he originally invented it some forty years earlier, which would place the date around 1839. Hills, more or less, accepts the statement by Ogden that he produced floating flies in 1839, but he tempers his enthusiasm by saying that forty years is a rather long wait before claiming such a significant contribution. There is nothing, however, to contradict what Ogden says to be so, and, as one of a family of flytiers, he introduced many excellent fly patterns, including some floaters.

In any event, by the 1840s the dry fly was in use in southern England and by the 1850s it was common.

The dry fly bloomed in all its glory until 1913, when Frederic Halford, who discussed its use extensively and exclusively in *Floating Flies and How to Dress Them* (1886), wrote his seventh and last book, *The*

Dry Fly Man's Handbook. Halford did not bring about the dry fly, but he was its champion and the spokesman for those who fished with floating flies. Until Halford's time the progress of the dry fly had been impeded by the lack of efficient tackle. With the advent of split-cane rods, oiled silk lines, lighter hooks, amadou to dry the fly, and paraffin to keep it afloat, the dry-fly cult surged forward. Two of Halford's fishing companions, George Selwyn Marryat and Henry Sinclair Hall, were responsible for the construction of the split-wing dry fly, in which sections were taken from a pair of wings rather than doubling a section in the same wing. This new technique produced a dry fly that cocked upright on the water and gave a much more balanced fly. Previously, the cast fly landed and floated on its side as often as upright, to the consternation of the caster. Additionally, in 1879 Marryat and Hall resolved another problem of the dry-fly fisher that was caused by the practice of tying the dry fly on an eyeless hook mounted on a short length of stiff gut. Not only was there a considerable amount of inflexibility in fishing with this gut, but in air-drying the fly by false casting it was subject to very rapid wear, and in a short amount of time the fly was useless. Marryat and Hall resolved the problem by redesigning the eyed hook that had been invented a half century earlier to the point where the dry fly could be dressed on it. Then, when the gut was worn from casting, it was simply cut and retied. Simple as it sounds today, this was probably the major factor contributing to the popularity of the dry fly.

It should be mentioned that although Halford reigned as the high priest of dry-fly fishing in England, he was not universally accepted by the angling fraternity and notably not by G. E. M. Skues, who fought this one-sided approach to fly fishing.

In 1890 Halford received a letter from Theodore Gordon inquiring about the dry fly, to which he responded most generously by sending a selection of his dry flies. For many this signifies the beginning of the dry fly in America, and a mystique has been built up around Theodore Gordon as the "father of the dry fly in America." This may be so, but more likely it is because we can easily document the event—the passing of the dry flies from England to America. There is evidence, however, of the dry fly being in use in America well before 1890. Gordon himself pointed out the passage in Thaddeus Norris' *American Angler* (1864), in which Norris relates, "By cracking the moisture from them between each throw, he would lay them so lightly on the glassy surface, that a brace of trout would take them at almost every cast, and before they sank or were drawn away. . . . Here was an exemplification of the advantage of keeping one's flies dry."

*Flies tied by Theodore Gordon in 1908–1909, from the John Alden Knight
collection.*

There is no question that this is dry-fly fishing, but it is with two
wet flies and not a fly specifically designed to float upright on the water.

In 1885 John Harrington Keene, of Greenwich, New York, put it
all together. In *American Sporting Periodicals of Angling Interest* by
Austin S. Hogan, published by the Museum of American Fly Fishing in
Manchester, Vermont, there is an excerpt from the fishing periodical
American Angler (August 18, 1885), in which Keene fully describes the
making of the dry fly. Later Keene put his thoughts in a book, *Fly-
Fishing and Fly-Making*, editions of 1887 and 1891, and thoroughly covered the manufacture of floating flies. Keene, incidentally, in his treatment of floating flies, even gets into a floating imitation of a June bug, a
terrestrial, and gives instructions on how to strip the herl from the eye of
a peacock feather and use it for a body on his Quill Gnat. The stripped
peacock-eye quill body that Keene describes is, of course, the same
body as Gordon used on his famous Quill Gordon. John McDonald's *The
Complete Fly Fisherman* (1949) carries Gordon's dressing on page 127 as
related by R. B. Marston in the *Fishing Gazette* (August 11, 1906).

In his reference to the second edition, 1891, Keene makes note of
his contribution: "Many works describing fly making in the land of Wal-

ton exist, but no practical flytier has hitherto attempted to specifically instruct the American fly fisherman. This work is intended to fill the vacant niche in the piscatorial library."

There were other writers besides Keene who touched upon dry-fly fishing before 1890. Genio C. Scott, in *Fishing in American Waters* (1869), gives explicit instructions on fly-tying materials that will float the fly, as "a floating lure is better than a sinking one." Scott, however, was still dealing with a cast of wet flies fished "dry." Others to mention the true dry fly before 1890 in America were M. C. Weidmeyer, *American Fish and How to Catch Them* (1885), Leroy Milton Yale (*Scribner's Magazine*, July 1892), and William C. Harris (*American Angler*, November 10, 1888).

In the early 1900s dry-fly fishing was radiating from a number of directions. William C. Harris' *The Trouts of America* (1902) was an early exposition on the use of the dry fly, as was Louis Rhead's *The Book of Fish and Fishing* (1908) and Edward Breck's *The Way of the Woods* (1908).

To my mind, Breck, who purchased some of his dry flies from Theodore Gordon, was particularly farsighted. This is what he says regarding the dry fly:

> It was inevitable that American fishermen should wish to transfer to their own waters this highest development of the art of angling, and many of us have practiced it here as we were taught on the Itchen or Test, but, so far as I have been able to gather, with indifferent success, at least in the waters of the north woods. . . . Another reason may be that hitherto, Americans have not been able to purchase dry flies tied in imitation of American insects but have been obliged to be content with English importations—a state of affairs hardly creditable to our tackle dealers.

Apparently Dr. Breck didn't get a copy of the catalog from the T. H. Chubb Rod Company of Post Mills, Vermont, that was listing floating flies as early as 1896 (the date of my only catalog) and probably earlier. Flies were sold at 11 cents each or $1.25 per dozen, and a number of the dressings listed were of American origin, as evidenced notably by Seth Green, Beaverkill, and Parmachene Belle.

In 1912, when Emlyn Gill wrote his *Practical Dry-Fly Fishing*, there was a substantial amount of interest in the dry fly and dry-fly fishing. Although Gill's book is the first American book completely devoted to the dry fly, it is a somewhat disappointing primer, which rehashes English methods and opinions. In his introduction Gill mentioned

George M. L. La Branche—"one of the very best of all-around American anglers"—and predicted that La Branche would shortly present his ideas to the angling public "at the proper time."

Samuel Camp's *Fishing with Floating Flies* appeared in 1913, and then, as predicted by Gill, George M. L. La Branche arrived on the scene like a lightning bolt. Not only was La Branche an expert dry-fly man, he was a purist! From La Branche's *Dry Fly and Fast Water* (1914) came new ideas and techniques that were applicable to American waters. Later on La Branche favored his followers with the application of his techniques to the Atlantic salmon in *The Salmon and the Dry Fly* (1924). Again, this was another novel book, although Theodore Gordon had tied dry flies for Atlantic salmon at a considerably earlier date.

Theodore Gordon, too, had left his disciples: Herman Christian, Roy Steenrod, inventor of the Hendrickson, and Reuben Cross. Cross claimed to have learned his fly-tying art from Theodore Gordon, but Herman Christian disputed this claim. In any event, as a prolific commercial tier, Cross did more than anyone else to popularize the now famous Quill Gordon.

The dry fly had captured the fancy of Edward R. Hewitt, who was fishing it for trout as early as 1906. It was Hewitt's inventive mind that developed the deadly Neversink Skater, the spider or variant form of the dry fly. In 1922, in *Secrets of the Salmon*, he wrote of the combined dry-fly experiences with salmon of Col. Ambrose Monell—"the best salmon fisherman I ever met"—and George M. L. La Branche.

Hendrickson, tied by Roy Steenrod, from the Ralph Daniels collection.

The Neversink Skater, tied by E. R. Hewitt, from the Ralph Daniels collection.

In 1916 Louis Rhead continued the interest in the dry fly with *American Trout-Stream Insects,* and George Holden came out with his informative *Streamcraft* in 1919. Rhead's book was the first serious approach to entomology for the fishermen. Rhead failed in that he did not relate the common names of insects with their scientific nomenclature. This wouldn't be successfully done until Preston Jennings' *Book of Trout Flies* in 1935.

Floating deer-hair flies were on the water and being fished for trout with Orley C. Tuttle's Devil Bug in 1915. Deer hair for flies was not new. As early as 1791, in *Travels Through North and South Carolina,* William Bartram mentioned using the "bob," a deer-hair-and-feather creation, in Florida. Peter Schwab extolled the floating qualities of the Emerson Hough, Van Luven Rogue, Myers Buck, and Queen Bess in *Outdoor Recreation* (August 1927). In 1929, while fishing the Ausable River in New York, Lee Wulff developed his Gray Wulff dry fly with deer-hair wings and tail in order to imitate some large gray-colored drakes. Little did he know then that this was to become one of the most popular dry flies of all time.

The dry fly had safely arrived in America. Not only did it find its champions among American anglers, but it changed its own identity so

The Gray Wulff, tied by Lee Wulff, from the A. I. "Pal" Alexander collection.

that it could excel on waters that were often swift or brush-lined; it was even sent on searching missions over the water, not to tempt a particular rising fish but on a blind search for any trout! To the English angler of the chalk streams it may have been heresy; to the American trout fisherman it soon became a way of life.

My Favorite Places to Fish	Type of Fish	Best Time	Suggested Flies — Type	Size
West Branch, Penobscot River, Maine	Landlocked salmon	Fall	1. Badger Spider 2. Adams 3. Light Cahill	12–14 12–14 12–14
Squannacook River, Massachusetts	Brown	Spring	1. March Brown 2. Quill Gordon 3. Ginger Quill	16 14–18 18–20
Miramichi River, New Brunswick, Canada	Atlantic salmon	Fall	1. Buck Bug 2. Gray Wulff 3. Badger Spider	10 10–12 10–12
Neversink River, New York	Brown	Spring	1. Green Drake 2. March Brown 3. Adams	8–10 14–18 14–16
Batten Kill River, Vermont	Brown	Spring and fall	1. Quill Gordon 2. Ginger Quill 3. Black Quill	16 18–20 18–20

Although he was born in West Virginia, Ed Zern has lived in New York since 1943 and has fished in England, Scotland, Ireland, Iceland, Spain, France, Norway, Kenya, Chile, Argentina, Ecuador, Yucatan, Brazil, Baja California, Peru, New Zealand, thirty-one U.S. states, and six Canadian provinces.

He is a past president of Theodore Gordon Flyfishers, the Westchester Retriever Field Trial Club, and the Advertising Sportsmen's Club of New York and a member of Trout Unlimited, the Federation of Fly Fishermen, Ducks Unlimited, the African Safari Club of New York, the Explorers, and a number of wildlife and resource-related conservation organizations. He has served as director of the American Motors Conservation Awards Program since its inception in 1953. Currently the fishing editor of Field & Stream, *he has written several books of outdoor humor and contributes to various other publications.*

3. Some Fish and Some Fishermen
A Few Anglers of Legend

Ed Zern

A POET GAVE GLORY to God for dappled things, including trout, presumably of all rose-stippled species. A lesser writer but a greater specifist, I thank God for brown trout, even though he shares my gratitude with Fred Mather, a fish culturist who, in the year 1883, undertook to remedy the Almighty's oversight in neglecting to provide North America with *Salmo trutta* (or *Salmo fario,* as fashion then had it). Mather, working in fairly unmysterious ways his wonders to perform, arranged to have 80,000 fertile brown trout eggs shipped into New York harbor by a German pisciculturist named Von Behr, which is why, in my early angling years, I would occasionally overhear a crusty codger seated on the bank of the Brodheads or Little Lehigh lament the passing of the "native trout" and the advent of "them goddam Von Behrs." More often the reference was simply to "them Germans."

"Them goddam Von Behrs" were, of course, not nearly as pretty as the native brook trout, nor were they quite as stupid. They were also much more able to cope with the changing water conditions—warming and silting of streams as watersheds were stripped of timber and pollution of lakes and streams as water-powered industries switched to other kinds of power but continued to use the waterways as God-given waste-disposal facilities. And so, gradually, the alien salmonids displaced or replaced the less adaptable native char; the village hotshot trout man, who had once flung gut-snelled, heavy-ironed Dusty Millers, Black Gnats, and Parmachene Belles into the local creek or river and returned to town with a gunnysack full of native trout, began coming home from the same water, now infested with unvermiculated, cannibalistic, and often infuriatingly pickier brown trout, with an empty creel.

Even today, in some benighted parts of the country, the brown is still frowned upon as an interloper. I recall stopping beside a roadside stretch of a Maine river—all right, it was (and still is, I suppose) the Sandy—on my way to fish Moosehead Lake for landlocked salmon, sometime in the early sixties, and thinking that it looked remarkably trouty. It was coming on evening and I had a fur piece still to drive, but I hastily rigged a rod, bent a fuzzy nymph that "Polly" Roseborough had given me on a 3X leader, and cast at the head of a rocky run. On the first drift a 17-inch brown took the fly, and I measured and released it. The second drift produced a 19-inch brown just under 3 pounds, which I kept because it was badly hooked and had taken so long to surrender that I didn't think it would survive if it were released. When I got to Moosehead Lake House, I tried to palm off the 19-incher on my guide, who recoiled as though I'd offered him a live Gaboon viper.

"Ye gawds, Ay-uhd," he protested, "thet's no propuh traout—thet's a braown!" He wasn't kidding, and I suspect a lot of native-born New Englanders would agree with him vehemently.

But the fact is if it were not for the introduction of Herr Von Behr's fish eggs and the subsequent importation of other strains of *Salmo trutta,* most notably from Britain, dry-fly fishing, as we know it today throughout most of the United States, would not exist. Not that our native species, the eastern brook and the western cutthroat and rainbow, won't deign to feed on floating insects, sometimes as voraciously as any

Brown replacing Brooks.

brown. They will indeed. I recall with considerable chagrin my then eleven-year-old son, Brook, taking 12- to 16-inch cutthroats on awkwardly cast dry flies from the south fork of the Flathead River in the Bob Marshall Wilderness Area of Montana almost literally hand-over-fist. His disappointment came later, when he expected every second or third cast of a dry fly to produce a respectable trout; on the Beaverkill or the Big Hole or the Green or the Deschutes that doesn't happen. No, the brown is a different customer and infinitely harder to bamboozle. Not for him the gaudy concoctions that beguile the squaretails in a Maine thoroughfare, nor the frowsy floaters that inveigle and vanquish the cutthroat cruising the flats of a back-country Wyoming river.

And without the brown trout there would be no Vince Marinaro or Charlie Fox, no Ernie Schwiebert or Len Wright, no George Harvey or Art Flick, no Richards and/or Swisher, no Dettes or Darbees, and almost certainly no size 20 or 24 flies, except perhaps as curios, nor any leaders finer than 4X. Lacking the brown trout there would have been no Preston Jennings, no Skip Wetzel, no Edward Hewitt, no George La Branche, no Theodore Gordon. None of them would have been necessary. In short, there would not be a great American tradition of dry-fly fishing, a tradition still developing and maturing despite growing pressures of population and pollution.

I thank you, God and Mr. Mather.

Most sports have champions or star performers or some variety of hero. But when we speak of sport, we usually mean not a true sport at all but a game—tennis, golf, baseball, football, track, or some other contest of one group of men, or one man, against another. (I recall being asked by a major television producer if I would like to be flown to Montana for a week of fishing the then little-known spring creeks of the Yellowstone. When I said I would like that very much, he said, "Splendid. You'll be fishing against Ted Trueblood—East versus West, y'know." I explained that I *didn't* know, that trout fishing was not a game or a competitive sport, and that Trueblood would certainly feel the same way, as of course he did. The producer got two other people, and the program, I'm happy to report, was a dismal bore.)

I'm thankful there are no "champion" fly fishermen (although there are champion fly casters whose skills and techniques I admire and envy and whose supremacy can be measured in feet and inches). But there have been, and are, outstanding trout fishermen, and the qualities that make them outstanding aren't measurable in feet of casting distance or pounds of trout or numbers of fish. All those I have known were fly fishermen first and foremost, but some were possessed of deadly skill with a minnow, and a few were whilom artists with the delicately cast upstream worm.

The qualities that make them outstanding are various: enthusiasm often amounting to dedication; intelligence, in a fundamental sense of the word; keen powers of observation; a knowledge of streams and the ability to read them and to know where fish should be in any conditions of water or weather; a high degree of skill in presenting the fly (although some of them seldom fished, or fish, a line-with-leader longer than twenty-five feet); a knowledge of aquatic insect life above, on, and under the water; a willingness to question traditional techniques, to experiment and innovate; a degree of articulateness in explaining or defending their inventions and innovations. Few of them have all those qualities, but many of them have most of them.

(I'm aware that this book is about *dry*-fly fishing, but I find it difficult to categorize the outstanding trout men I've known into dry-fly fishermen or wet-fly fishermen or nymph fishermen. Most of them, like Ernest Schwiebert, George Harvey, Joe Brooks, A. J. McClane, Preston Jennings, John Alden Knight, and Larry Madison, to name a few, were skillful dry-fly fishers who were equally adept with nymphs and streamers when the occasion arose.)

From about 1935 to 1945 I fished Brodheads Creek nearly every weekend of the season, which then ran from April 1 to July 31; I also spent most of my summer vacations at Charley Rethoret's Hotel Rapids at Analomink, which was also my weekend headquarters. There I was fortunate to meet, and occasionally to fish with, a number of distinguished anglers: Eugene Connett, who published Derrydale Press books at prices I couldn't afford; George La Branche, who generally stayed at a private club up the river but who not infrequently dropped into the hotel for lunch or dinner or to bend a friendly elbow with other anglers at the bar (Charley had been a chef at Chalfonte-Haddon Hall in Atlantic City before buying the Hotel Rapids, and his food was as irresistible as his beds were unsleepable); Art Neu, a professional and world champion fly caster who tutored me occasionally, although not to much avail; Preston Jennings, a kindly man willing to share his immense knowledge and enthusiasm with anyone of kindred tastes; John Alden Knight, inventor of the Solunar Tables and the Mickey Finn Bucktail, with whom I later spent some pleasant days fishing the Loyalsock, the Young Womans, and other Pennsylvania freestone streams; "Big Jim" Leisenring, a gentle man and fellow Pennsylvania Dutchman, who taught me to fish a wet fly with a true dead drift and who, so far as I know, never fished anything but the sparsely dressed wet flies for which he was famous, no matter how many trout were rising to surface insects (and who took one hell of a lot of trout); Bache Brown, who introduced the spinning rod and reel to America commercially, and I suppose if he hadn't, someone else would have; Richard Salmon, whose recently published limited-edition volume on flies and fly-tying, with actual materials instead of illustrations, is a delight.

I might have amounted to something as a trout fisherman if I had spent more time cultivating the famous anglers who frequented Charley's inn. Instead I spent every minute I could on the water, and for the first four years of my Brodheads angling I scorned wets and nymphs and streamers, using only dries from opening day to the end of the season. I pretended to be a hard-nosed purist, but the fact is I simply didn't know how to fish a wet fly or a nymph or a streamer properly. With the floating fly I could *see* what was happening (which was usually that the fly was dragging badly and putting down trout for yards around), and somehow I took trout often enough on the dries, even in the midst of several opening-day snowstorms, to be able to convince myself that there was a modicum of method in my madness.

Since I then knew next to nothing about hatches, much less how to match them, I fished all one season using nothing but Quill Gordons and Light Cahills in various sizes and another season using nothing but

Ed Zern fishing hatch with oversize pattern.

Wickham's Fancys. I spent almost no time trying to decide which pattern to use or changing from one pattern to another. As a result, my fly was on the water a good bit of the time, and I caught a considerable number of trout, mostly stocked fish but occasionally one I judged to be wild or at least to be a carry-over.

I had never heard of Edward Hewitt at that time, but for several seasons I relied heavily on an invention of his—the bivisible—which produced some excellent catches.

We are, of course, all indebted to Hewitt, and not merely for the bivisible or for his lovely skater on which, fishing it downstream one June afternoon a lot of years ago, I hooked fifteen brown trout just below Cook's Falls on the Beaverkill; I kept six between 16 and 17 inches. Hewitt, a man born to wealth and privilege, used the former to acquire some of the finest brown trout water in the eastern United States and to make a number of experiments involving tackle and tactics, artificial feeding, stream improvement, and propagation, all of which provided valuable information to professional and amateur trout culturists and to all serious fly fishers. He was a highly opinionated man and was sometimes wrong in his conclusions, but if he lacked the dispassionate objectivity of the trained scientist, he approached fly fishing and its related problems with enthusiasm and a genuinely creative intelligence.

When Preston Jennings, who spent most of his time when I knew him collecting specimens of aquatic insects in various stages and fished infrequently, found out that my wife was more fascinated by the life cycles of mayflies and stone flies and caddises than were most of the fishermen at Charley's, he spent many hours showing her the larvae and nymphs of the most important insect species in the Brodheads. For years to come I relied on Evelyn's identifications when checking the undersides of rocks along a river bank. Jennings' *A Book of Trout Flies*, published by Connett's Derrydale Press in 1935, was the first serious effort to identify and sort out on some kind of scientific basis the aquatic insect life that provides trout forage in eastern American streams. Despite its limited range and some doubtful identifications, the book was of vast importance to anyone concerned with the development of fly fishing and fly-tying.

Some years later Bill Bueno, a book editor, invited me to have lunch with him and a young, gifted architectural student, Ernest Schwiebert, who had written a book called *Matching the Hatch*, then still in manuscript form. Having found that neither Charles Wetzel's *Practical Fly Fishing* nor Art Flick's *Streamside Guide* had been of much value when I fished the rivers of western Montana and Wyoming, since these books were limited to rivers of the eastern seaboard, my chief contribution to the discussion was to suggest to the young man that the western flies (which he had covered fairly thoroughly) should be put into a special section. The book has become a bible to serious fly fishermen both East and West and covers far more ground more accurately than Jennings, Wetzel, or Flick has done. And Ernie Schwiebert has become almost a legend along the Letort and other Pennsylvania limestoners because of his skill in extracting outsize browns from difficult lies.

In 1941, I think it was, I drove from Philadelphia to the town of Boiling Springs, Pennsylvania, to find and fish the Yellow Breeches, about which I knew nothing except that its name intrigued me. I was surprised and pleased to find almost in the center of the village a lake of several acres formed by enormous springs that bubbled up through the sandy bottom, creating a sort of boiling effect and giving rise to the Yellow Breeches. I arrived in midafternoon on a bright June day and noticed several local fishermen sitting back in the shade of some trees near the lake, content to watch a score or more of rising trout, some of them obviously in the 3-to-5-pound class.

It was clear to me that the locals were unable to cope with the situation, and that I, having cut my fly-fishing teeth on the difficult Brodheads browns, should show them how. I parked the car, got into my Anderson waders and muleskin brogues, set up an 8-foot Hardy rod with a Hardy "Uniqua" reel and silk HDH line, tied on a standard 9-foot 4X leader to which I added two 20-inch 4X tippets, tied the terminal to a size 18 Adams, and stepped into the gin-clear water prepared to show the yokels how a city slicker catches trout when a farmer can't. The yokels were obviously willing to learn, as they continued to sit in the shade and watch my preparations.

Forty minutes later, after I had changed flies ten or twelve times and cast to rising trout until my arm ached, it occurred to me that perhaps the farmers knew something; I reeled in and walked up to one who looked fairly civilized. "That's tough fishing," I said.

"It is indeed," said the local. "Sometimes, if the sun goes under a cloud, you can fool one of those babies—that's what we're waiting for, a cloud or two. Even then, though, it's difficult. What size fly are you using?"

"Eighteens and twenties," I said, figuring he would never have heard of flies that tiny.

"You'd be better off with twenty-twos or twenty-fours," the yokel said, gently. "What size tippet do you have on?"

"I've been fishing about twelve feet of leader, to Four-X," I said,

Brown refusal.

thinking that this guy wouldn't know about Xs but only about pound tests.

"Even when it's overcast you won't do much with Four-X," the man said. "Mostly we use Six-X, although sometimes you can get by with Five-X—and I like to have at least fifteen feet of leader behind it. Tell you what: why don't we go down the road a piece and try the river there—might be some trout working under the banks. I can see you've come some distance, and you might as well get some fishing. I'll be happy to show you around."

I said I'd be most grateful, and in a few minutes we were wading a lovely dry-fly stretch of the Breeches. My mentor had a sinkbucket tied to his belt in which he put the six or seven nice browns he quickly took on a Ginger Quill, while I was still working on my first fish. "I live on a little river called the Letort," he explained, "and I'm doing some experimental stocking. Would you like to come with me while I run these fish over to my water?"

When I said I'd like to stay and fish until dark but was staying at the local inn, we arranged to meet in the morning. He said, "Well, good luck. By the way, my name's Fox. Charlie Fox." We fished the next day, and I went back to Philadelphia realizing I had met a master fisherman and an exceptional human being, although it was some time before I came across any of his writings. Through Charlie I met Vince Marinaro and a number of other denizens of the limestone creek area near Carlisle that produces some of the most skillful fly fishers in the world, simply because no other kind is able to take fish consistently from the weedy, slow-flowing limestone waters of Pennsylvnia. Marinaro's *Modern Dry-Fly Code*, published in 1950, is a true angling classic, and his new book, *In the Ring of the Rise* (1976), is perhaps even more important. In the former Marinaro introduced the concept of tiny flies—from size 20 to size 28—for big trout and pointed out the importance of terrestrials in the diet of meadow-stream trout and of their imitations, particularly the various jassids. His new book takes it from there.

George Harvey, now retired from his professorship at Penn State, where he taught a full-credit course in fly fishing to more than 7,000 students over a period of four decades, is one of the most skillful fly fishers I have ever known. It has been my privilege to spend many pleasant and instructive days with him on the limestone streams of central Pennsylvania and many hours at his tying bench, watching him turn out the most perfectly tied small flies I have ever seen. It's George's theory, which I'm convinced is correct, that the leader tippet, no matter how heavy, doesn't deter trout from taking a fly, and that the term "gut-shy," in reference to superwary trout, should in fact be "drag-shy." Admittedly, a heavy leader is more likely to cause drag than a lighter leader, but George, who adjusts the length of his leader and tippet each time he changes flies, has learned to present the dry fly with the leader in coils or curves that ensure at least a few feet of dragfree drift—an easier cast to write about than to make, but one that takes gut-shy trout on a 3X or even a 2X tippet if properly done.

I can't imagine how I got this far without mentioning one of the giants, Lee Wulff, with whom I've fished for trout and salmon and shot a

Wulff dry fly.

few grouse and woodcock. If Lee had done nothing more than develop the Wulff flies—and he has done immensely more, with pen and paintbrush and camera as well as in the development of tackle and techniques—he would have been assured of angling immortality and a place in the heart of every fisherman who has ever had a 5-pound trout or a 20-pound salmon rise and take a floating White or Gray Wulff.

And then, of course, there's . . . , but I'm way over my word limit.

My Favorite Places to Fish	*Type of Fish*	*Best Time*	*Suggested Flies*	
			Type	*Size*
Brodheads Creek, Eastern Pennsylvania	Brown	May–June	1. Quill Gordon 2. Light Cahill 3. Hendrickson	14 14–16 12–14
Test and/or Itchen rivers and tributaries, Hants, England	Brown	June–July	Depending on hatches	
Madison River, Beaverhead, etc., Montana	Brown Rainbow	First week in July	Sofa pillow	6
Irisiburn River Te Anau South Island New Zealand	Brown	January– February	Royal Wulff	16
Spruce Creek, Central Pennsylvania	Brown	July– September	Caenis imitations and various terrestrials	18–22
Cumilahue River, Chile	Brown	January	Various dries	12–18

Poul Jorgensen is one of the best-known names in American fly fishing. He is an expert fisherman, a well-known conservationist, an innovative flytier, a lecturer, and a writer.

He is an active officer in such organizations as the American League of Anglers, the Theodore Gordon Flyfishers, and Trout Unlimited. He is also a trustee of the Museum of American Fly Fishing and a director of the Brotherhood of the Jungle Cock.

He is the author of Dressing Flies for Fresh and Salt Water, *of Poul Jorgensen's* Trout Fly Charts, *and* Modern Fly Dressings for the Practical Angler.

Born in Denmark, Jorgensen settled in the United States more than twenty years ago and now lives in Towson, Maryland.

4. The Dry Fly
Basic Imitations with
Their Dressings

Poul Jorgensen

I RECENTLY RECEIVED a copy of a delightful book on fly-tying by Dr. Preben Torp Jacobsen, a Danish angler-author who is also one of Europe's leading fly dressers. In it he says, "Even though the fly is the smallest and least expensive part of a fly fisher's gear, I am not totally wrong in saying that it's also close to being the most important." I think the author's view is shared by most of us, even though many anglers will surely argue that skillful presentation ranks equal in importance, and I, for one, agree that this may be so. But even a good presentation cannot overcome the handicap of a dry fly that does not float properly and fails to fool the fish into believing it is the real thing; namely, an insect.

When an angler has learned to use his fly rod and is able to cast upstream so that the dry fly floats downstream without drag, he has only won half the battle, and for the dry-fly fisherman in particular it is just the beginning. To be truly successful in his sport, he must learn about the insects upon which the fish are feeding and be able to identify a few of them so that he can choose an artificial that closely matches the natural in size, color, and shape. To the novice this may sound like a lot of trouble, and to a few it may even appear as if dry-fly fishing were so difficult that it was designed only for the enjoyment of a few people with special talents. Of course, this is not so, and one doesn't have to be an entomologist to learn about the happenings at streamside. I, for one, couldn't care less about the reason why a fish will take a tiny midge-sized fly and ignore a large juicy grasshopper, as long as I am able to match the midge being taken. As a fly dresser, however, I am concerned about the insects I am imitating, not only for the sake of iden-

Typical dry flies.

tification but for the purpose of choosing the right proportions, materials, hook, and tying method.

Most of the dry flies you see are representatives of three basic groups of adult insects: mayflies, caddis flies, and terrestrials and at times some less important insects, mostly of local interest, including the midges. They are all dressed and fished differently but have one thing in common; the fish take them on the surface, and the flies that imitate them, therefore, must float.

MAYFLY IMITATIONS

For the fly fisher, the mayfly would be first on the list if one were to rate insects in order of their importance. Most dry flies are dressed to imitate these beautiful insects, including Theodore Gordon's famous Quill Gordon, a fly that has set a standard in style and method of dressing for dozens of the old classics still in use today.

Mayflies are easy to recognize by their long, slim bodies, with two or three long, thin tails and rather large wings, which are held upright when the insect is at rest. Since there may be many different mayflies hatching on the same stream during the day and evening, each of a different color and size, it is important for the angler to recognize the ones hatching on the water or swarming in the air at the time he is fishing and to try to match them with an artificial. The flies to use during a hatch are those with upright wings resembling the freshly emerged duns floating on the stream. They look like little sailboats while they are drying their wings. Later, when the flies have completed their second transformation or molt, mating and egg-laying takes place over the stream. With this the life cycle of a precious insect has been completed. When the exhausted and dying spinners fall on the water with their wings spread out, the fish go on another feeding binge.

The dry flies created to imitate the spinners are called spentwing flies. They are dressed with their wings extending out from the sides of the thorax instead of being set upright. The most famous of the traditional spent-wings is the Adams, which undoubtedly has been responsible for long strings of fish, but any of the well-known flies can be dressed to represent spinners. My personal favorite, however, is explained in one of my books on fly-tying (*Dressing Flies for Fresh and Salt Water*, Freshet Press, 1973) and is based on an idea by the prominent English angler James Cecil Mottram. In his book *Fly-fishing: Some New Arts & Mysteries* (1914) he briefly describes the silhouette Olive Duns, one of which has no hackle and is designed to float on its fur body, calling them "Flies of the Future." These interesting flies are easy to dress by merely attaching and splaying the horizontal tail, then winding a dry-fly hackle in front and shaping it into spentwings with figure-eight windings before applying a fur body and thorax.

Most of the dry flies that are used today imitate a specific insect, which does not mean it can only be used when that particular insect is on the water. For example, many anglers have found that while the Light Cahill, which represents the lightest cream-colored insect in the *Stenonema* group, is usually dressed on sizes 12 to 14, it is also a very good representative for many other of the smaller cream-colored insects tied on size 16 to 28 hooks.

CADDIS FLY IMITATIONS

The flies that have received the most publicity in recent years are caddis dry flies. Caddis have, of course, been around for many years, but not until Leonard M. Wright, Jr., wrote his highly acclaimed books, *Fishing the Dry Fly as a Living Insect* and, later, *Fly-fishing Heresies*, did these flies mature from second-class citizens to prominent, established fish-getters. Since Wright's books on effectively fishing and tying the caddis were published, many patterns of similar types have been popular.

The adult caddis flies or sedges, as they are often called, look much like moths. They are best recognized when at rest by their rather long wings, which lay parallel with the much shorter body and form a tent-like shape.

Two of the most popular patterns were designed by Larry Solomon, a prominent New York City angler, who, after a close study of the insect's behavior, decided that there had to be two different patterns. The first represents the adult caddis fly as it flutters and skims over the surface of the water. The second fly was designed to imitate a disabled insect that, for one reason or another, is unable to get off the water. They are both dressed with a fur body and no tails. The difference lies in the wing structure. The fluttering imitation has a wing of either deer hair or guard hairs from a mink's tail, tied down-wing, lying flat over the body and extending a full body length beyond the hook bend. When the wing is completed, a traditional dry-fly hackle is applied and wound over the wing butts in front. The second fly is called the delta-wing pattern and has a pair of hackle tips set flat instead of the hair, one on each side of the body at a 45-degree angle. Both of these flies are good floaters and can be tied in many different sizes and color combinations. The method of tying the flies are included in my latest book, *Modern Fly Dressings for the Practical Angler* (Winchester Press, 1976).

MIDGES

There are times when trout will refuse to take anything but speck-sized insects that you can't even see. Several summers ago, when fishing a pool on the famous Beaverkill River in the New York Catskills, my notes from previous trips indicated that I should fish a size 16 or 18 Blue-winged Olive. The fish apparently didn't read my notes, because they repeatedly refused to take my offerings, even though they were studying them. I watched from the grassy bank while repairing a leader and saw fish rising. It was a slow, sipping rise, but fish were feeding.

I've had similar experiences on the Yellow Breeches in Boiling Springs, Pennsylvania, during the late afternoon hours, before the evening appearance of blizzard hatches of the whitefly in August and September. There the fish will feed freely on a tiny cream midge that is so small that a size 32 hook would be too large. The Beaverkill fish have the same tastes. When I floated a size 28 midge with an olive fur body and only one turn of hackle over a feeding lane, a nice trout rose and sipped the fly. My theory of not needing the speck-sized artificials had been shattered. Although midge-tying is not my favorite pastime, I dressed a dozen artificials in olive, cream, and black for the next day; I will never be without them again!

TERRESTRIALS (LAND INSECTS)

There is little doubt that terrestrial fishing started in Pennsylvania. The limestone streams around Carlisle and Chambersburg wind slowly through pastures and meadows, and the famed Letort Spring Creek and others were the testing grounds for many successes and failures. An abundance of crickets, hoppers, ants, and beetles appear in midsummer, and the meadows are full of insect life. Vince Marinaro and Charles K. Fox, two of America's leading authorities on terrestrials and their imitation, have shared their early experiences with fellow anglers, and it is they who are largely responsible for the extended dry-fly season we all enjoy. Perhaps the most famous of all the creations is Vince's Jassid. It is dressed with a jungle cock nail laid flat over a spiraled hackle that has been trimmed on top and bottom so that it floats in the surface film, not on it. Since Jassids imitate the many tiny beetle and leaf-hopper-type insects, they are best in sizes 18 through 24 and can be dressed in many colors.

THE MECHANICS OF A DRY FLY

Even though it is beyond the scope of this chapter to venture too deeply into the arts and mysteries of fly-dressing techniques, there are a few basic points about a dry fly's construction that the angler should know, even if he doesn't tie his own flies. All of us will admit that the most important quality in a dry fly is its ability to float, and even the worst-looking or most poorly tied fly will catch fish now and then if it can be kept on the surface. It used to be that a dry fly was not authentic unless it was dressed in the traditional style, with the tightly bunched tail extending straight back about a body length and with a vertical floating hackle of the finest quality set in a collar around two upright and divided wings. A well-dressed dry fly of this type should meet certain standards of quality. The wings should be sitting on top of the hook shank and should be evenly divided at a 45-degree angle, with each wing having the same outward angle to its respective side of the body. The old method of testing the quality of the hackle still works. The stiffness can be tested by lightly pressing the hackle tips against the sensitive skin on your lips. If the hackle is good, you should feel the points.

Famous flies like the Adams, Quill Gordon, Royal Coachman, and many others of traditional vintage are still dressed that way. They float high, with the body and hook out of the water, resting on the tips of their hackle and tail; I am sure these imitations still catch most of the fish. But there has been a significant change in fly patterns in the last decade or two. A yearning for self-expression among flytiers has started this new trend not only in the newer generations but among many of the "older" established clique as well.

The down-the-middle-of-the-road discipline and the traditional methods of tying have been seriously challenged and, I might add, quite successfully. As advocated in classic books on dry-fly fishing, dry flies are no longer required to float high on their stiff hackle fibers. Many are designed to float on their fur bodies, stabilized by a splayed tail or a parachute hackle wound at the base of the wing; some have no hackle at all. This development, however, should not be interpreted as a cancellation of tradition, for that is surely here to stay, as much a part of dry-fly fishing as fishing itself. Nor does it mean a cancellation of the fly-tying basics handed down to us through generations. What it does mean is that we are widening horizons and making this sport more interesting, and for that there is always room.

There is one thing we cannot change and that is the basic ingredients which make a fly float. First, the finished fly must be as light as possible and dressed on fine light-wire hooks. These are manufactured specifically with dry flies in mind and come in many sizes from the largest size 4s to the smallest size 28s. Since the fly dresser must try to imitate many kinds of insects with varied dimensions, the manufacturers of hooks offer the above-mentioned sizes in regular, short, or long shank models, but they never forget that hooks must be made from the lightest wire possible.

I have often been asked if the obvious presence of a hook will discourage fish from striking. Since most terrestrial imitations and the new fly patterns that float on their body with the hook clearly visible underwater have proven to be very effective, I am now more than ever convinced that a showing hook is of little consequence. Furthermore, I have noticed that feeding fish will pick up a lot of trash such as small pieces of wood and bits of plants only to spit them out when they realize that this debris is not edible. They probably intend to do likewise with many artificial flies that they are tricked into taking, but instead they get hooked.

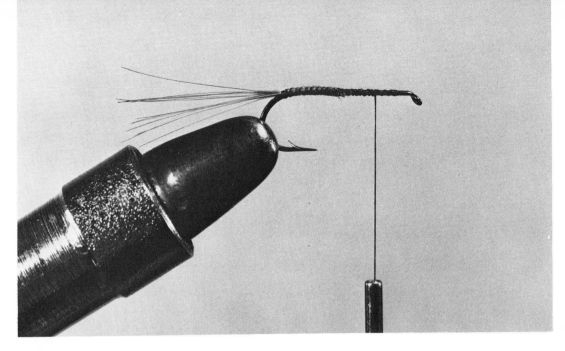

DRESSING A SIMPLE DRY FLY

Tie in six to eight stiff hackle fibers about the same length as the total hook length. Then wind the thread forward to the wing position, approximately a third of a hook length from the eye.

Fasten the wing material as shown, with the tips that form the wing pointing forward over the hook eye. The wing should also be about the same length as the total hook length.

Trim away the surplus wing material and fasten the ends on the shank with a few windings. Now lift the wing tips to an upright position and take several turns of thread directly in front of them. Divide the fibers into two equal bunches and apply some crisscross winding to keep them separate. A little cement will help secure the winding if you wish.

Wind the tying thread to the rear and apply enough fur dubbing on the thread to form the body. Try to make it a little tapered.

Wind the dubbing on the hook shank to form a body that comes just short of the wing. Tie in two good stiff dry-fly hackles, as seen. The fiber length in the middle of the hackles should be about 1½ hook gaps for good balance when floating.

Wind the hackles on edge in back and in front of the wing—one at a time gives the best result. Tie them off in front as they are wound and form a small head before applying a whip finish or a couple of half hitches. Some varnish or regular head cement will prevent the windings from unraveling. This finishes a simple dry fly.

There is one interesting observation, however, regarding flies that float on their fur body. I took some photographs of this type of fly from underwater, so that I could observe their appearance. I noticed that if the fly was dressed on a down-eyed hook, the eye would be in the surface film or slightly under and would cause a distorted "broken mirror" image of the fly. For this reason I now dress this kind of fly on up-eyed hooks, and they prove to have no distorted effect.

The next important thing to know about the construction of dry flies is that they must be dressed in the right proportions and with the best hackle and other material that can be obtained (see photographs of the Quill Gordon). The biggest problem today is obtaining good hackle; there just isn't enough of it to go around. Eric Leiser, a well-known fly dresser and material specialist, recently wrote an entire book on the subject of material for fly-tying called *Fly Tying Materials, Their Procurement, Use, and Protection* (Crown Publishers, 1973), in which he covers all materials, including those essential for dressing a good dry fly. I highly recommend this book for fishermen who have a desire to broaden their knowledge on this subject, but even with all the knowledge gained by reading books and getting catalogs from various supply houses, it is still difficult to get good dry-fly material. It used to be that a few people raised their own birds and would part with some super necks. But now it is too costly for most fanciers to raise special birds, and we are compelled to be satisfied with feathers that are available commercially, mostly imports from India. I believe we are going to see many more flies in the future that are designed without hackle, and, as with many of the terrestrials that are dressed with good-floating deer hair, the contemporary flytier will find new ways of using synthetics and other material for his "flies of the future."

A SELECTION OF DRY FLIES

If you were to ask a dozen anglers to list their choice of dry flies for all-around fishing in various parts of the country, it is certain that you would have twelve different lists. First, there is a big difference between the flies of the East and those that are used on the large, fast rivers of the West. Eastern anglers prefer sparsely dressed flies such as the Quill Gordon, small Adams, and Red Quills, as opposed to the Westerner, who likes his flies heavily dressed and prefers the Humpy, the Wulff, and the trimmed deer-hair flies, which are much better suited for the kind of water he fishes. The only common choice would be the terrestrials and midges that have proven their worth in all parts of the country. The method of dressing the flies in the following list is a

Spentwing Adams.   Realistic March Brown.

matter of preference. The individual can better decide what is best for him. Please note that my list of flies is by no means conclusive but merely contains suggestions for imitations that will take fish almost anywhere in the world.

MAYFLY AND CADDIS IMITATIONS

Adams. A gray fly that is considered one of the best that has ever been devised. It is often fished as a fluttering caddis but does not represent anything in particular. It can be fished all year, anywhere.

Hook: Size 10 to 20
Thread: Black
Tail: Brown and grizzly fibers
Body: Gray muskrat fur
Wings: Grizzly hackle tips, upright or spent
Hackle: Brown and grizzly wound together

American March Brown. One of the largest and best-known trout flies in America. It represents a specific insect (*Stenonema vicarium*) that appears in mid-May through mid-June on most eastern and midwestern streams. It can be dressed traditionally, no hackle, or cutwing parachute style. The best-known is the traditional dressing listed below.

Hook: Size 10 to 12
Thread: Orange
Tail: Dark ginger hackle fibers
Body: Fawn-colored fox fur—light
Wings: Wood duck flank feather
Hackle: Grizzly and ginger wound together

Bivisible. The bivisible is one of several flies that do not represent anything in particular. It can be dressed in any color and size, but all sizes are finished with a turn or two of white hackle, regardless of what color fly you have chosen. The late Edward R. Hewitt once said, "If you see no flies, tie on a size 12 bivisible. It seems to attract the trout when there are no hatches on the water."

Hook: Size 8 to 14
Thread: Black
Tail: Hackle fibers, same color as body hackle
Body: Palmered full length
Front: One or two turns of white hackle

Black Gnat. This is another fly that is not a representative of any particular insect, other than black flies in general. It used to be fished only in the larger sizes 10 and 12, but anglers have found that the smaller 16 to 24, and even size 28 midges, are very effective at times. The smaller sizes are generally dressed without wings.

Hook: Size 8 to 28
Thread: Black
Tail: Black hackle fibers
Body: Black chenille
          Note: I prefer to use black fur instead, as it is more water resistant.
Wings: Dark gray duck quill sections
Hackle: Black

Black Quill—Whirling Dun. This fly can be used both in the East and in the Midwest. I have found it best in sizes 10 to 12, at least early in the season, but smaller sizes down to 22 are also effective when very small grayish insects are on the water.

Hook: Sizes 10 to 22
Thread: Black
Tail: Blue dun hackle fibers
Body: Stripped peacock quill
Wings: Gray duck quill sections
Hackle: Blue dun

Blue-wing Olive—Small Dun Variant (Flick). This fly is very important in the East when dressed as recommended by Art Flick, who dresses it in variant style. It has also been used successfully throughout the country dressed with regular size hackle. It is a very good representative of most of the olive-colored Baetis flies. This fly can be fished all year round, also as a tiny midge.

Hook: Size 16 to 28
Thread: Olive
Tail: Natural dark blue dun fibers
Body: Olive yarn pulled apart and mixed with a small amount of muskrat fur. Body must be very small with a distinct olive cast.

Cream Variant (Flick). There are few flies that are more important than this fairly large imitation. It can be dressed in any size and fished whenever cream-colored insects are on the water.

Hook: Size 12 to 20, short shank
Thread: Yellow
Tail: Long cream hackle fibers
Body: Stripped cream hackle stem
Hackle: Cream, tied variant style

Dun Variant (Flick). This fly represents the evening hatches of the largest smoky gray insects (*Isonychia bicolor*). Before Art Flick introduced the Variant, the favorite flies were the White-gloved Howdy and the Coachman—two flies we don't see much of anymore, except perhaps the wet Coachman, which is excellent.

Hook: Size 10 to 12, short shank
Tail: Dark blue dun hackle fibers
Body: Stripped quill stem from a red cock hackle
Hackle: Dark blue dun hackle

Bivisible.   *Irresistible.*

Delta-Wing Caddis (Solomon). Imitations of the fluttering insects in the Trichoptera family have reached a peak in popularity in recent years. The delta-wing pattern imitates an injured insect and can be dressed in almost any size and color combination to resemble the naturals on streams anywhere and can be fished all year around.

Hook: Size 14 to 22
Thread: Black
Body: Fur or Seal-Ex dubbing
Wings: Two hackle tips
Hackle: Wound dry-fly style over wing butts in front
           Note: Color of body, wing, and hackle selected to match those
           of insect being imitated.

Goofus Bug. This Western deer-hair fly is also referred to as the Humpy and is regarded as one of the best Western patterns ever devised. In the larger sizes they are often used for salmon, but the most popular ones are dressed in sizes 8 to 16.

Hook: Size 8 to 16
Thread: Black
Tail: Moose body hair
Body: Deer body hair
Wings: Deer body hair
Hackle: Grizzly and brown, wound together

Gray Fox Variant. This fly imitates the Green Drake, an insect known by most dry-fly anglers who are serious about their sport. The Green Drake is one of the largest insects, and the oversized hackles of multiple color or several different shades of hackle wound together make for a very effective artificial.

Hook: Size 10 to 12, short shank
Thread: Primrose
Tail: Ginger hackle fibers, fairly long
Body: Stripped cream or light ginger hackle stem
Hackle: One light ginger, one dark ginger, and one grizzly hackle

Skater. This interesting fly was designed in the 1930s by Edward R. Hewitt for trout fishing on his beloved Neversink River in New York State but later it proved very effective for salmon on North American rivers. It's similar to variant-type flies with its oversize hackle, but it has neither tail nor body—just two large hackles would dry-fly style and pressed closely together to form a disklike affair that often is several

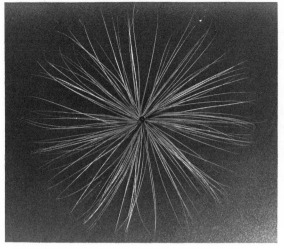

Hewitt Skater.   *Wulff hairwing.*

inches in diameter. It can be dressed in almost any color and is fished by skating it over the surface of the water like a natural insect. The hook that is best suited for these flies has a short shank with an upturned eye, sizes 8 to 12.

Gray Wulff. Lee Wulff, a great American angler, designed this fly in 1930 to represent many of the gray flies on the stream. It is one of many Wulff flies that have since proven effective when fishing the big, fast rivers of the West, as well as other waters, for trout, salmon, bass, and sunfish.

Hook: Size 4 to 14
Thread: Black
Tail: Natural brown bucktail
Body: Blue-gray wool
Wings: Natural brown bucktail
Hackle: Two blue-gray saddle hackles

Hairwing Caddis. This fly represents the fluttering caddis and can be tied in many different color combinations.

Hook: Size 14 to 22
Thread: Black
Body: Fur or Seal-Ex dubbing
Wings: Mink tail guard hair or deer body hair
Hackle: Wound dry-fly style over the wing butts in front

Note: Color of body, wing, and hackle selected to match those of insect being imitated.

Hendrickson. This dry fly was designed by Roy Steenrod, of Liberty, New York, in 1916, and it has been popular ever since. It's primarily an Eastern pattern and was meant to imitate the female species of *Ephemerella invaria* that appears on the stream in early spring.

Hook: Size 12 to 14
Thread: Tan
Tail: Blue dun hackle fibers
Body: Fawn-colored fur from red box belly
Wings: Wood duck flank feather
Hackle: Rusty blue dun hackle

Irresistible. The Irresistible is a well-known, trimmed deer-hair fly that is used in both the East and the West. It can be dressed in many sizes and different color combinations, but perhaps one of the best is described in the dressing below. Like the famous Wulff patterns, the Irresistible is effective for trout, salmon, bass, and sunfish.

Hook: Size 4 to 14
Thread: Black
Tail: Brown deer hair
Body: Deer body hair trimmed to shape
Wings: Brown deer hair
Hackle: Dark blue dun

Light Cahill. If there were one fly you would not want to be without, it would be the Light Cahill. It can be tied in any size to represent some of the many cream-colored insects found on most trout streams.

Hook: Size 12 to 24
Thread: Pale yellow
Tail: Cream or light ginger
Body: Cream fur
Wings: Palest wood duck flank feather
Hackle: Cream or lightest ginger

Quill Gordon. Being the most famous dry fly in America, it really deserves a whole book by itself. It was designed by Theodore Gordon to imitate *Epeorus pleuralis*, which is well distributed on Eastern streams.

Hook: Size 12 to 14
Thread: Black
Tail: Blue dun hackle fibers
Body: Stripped peacock quill, light
Wings: Wood duck flank feather
Hackle: Blue dun

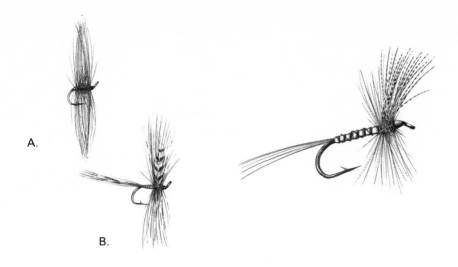

A. *Skater.* B. *Variant.*   *Quill Gordon.*

Red Quill. The Catskill fly dressers have fostered many famous American dry flies, and one of the best is the Red Quill, imitating the male *Ephemerella subvaria*, of which the Hendrickson, mentioned earlier, is the female. It can be tied in any size to represent some of the small, dark insects on the stream, but the original intention for imitating the specific insect was to dress it in sizes 12 to 14.

Hook: Size 12 to 14
Thread: Black
Tail: Blue dun
Body: Stripped brown hackle stem
Wings: Wood duck flank feather
Hackle: Medium blue dun

Royal Coachman. For not representing anything in particular, the Royal Coachman has done well indeed. It is not only an effective fly in almost any size, but it has quickly become the best-known dry fly in the world.

Hook: Size 10 to 20
Thread: Black
Tail: Golden pheasant tippet
Body: Peacock herl with red floss center band
Wings: White duck quill sections or calf tail hair
Hackle: Dark coachman—brown

TERRESTRIAL IMITATIONS

Ants. The best and most recognized imitations are also the simplest. Most terrestrials are poor swimmers, and ants need not float high on the

Royal Coachman.   (left) *Black Ant.* (right) *Jassid.*

water like traditional dry flies but are fished much better in the surface
film. The black ant and the red ant in any size, even the smallest 28s are
two of the most effective patterns.

Hook: Size 10 to 28
Thread: Black
Body: Two clumps of fur, the rear larger than the front
Hackle: Tied sparsely between the two fur clumps and trimmed top
          and bottom
          Note: Color of material chosen to match the insect being imi-
          tated.

Black Beetle. On many trout streams there is no fly that works better
than a Black Beetle. They blow into the water on windy days or simply
fall into the water, and trout love them.

Hook: Size 14 to 20
Thread: Black
Body: Tying thread over deer body hair
Legs: Black deer body hair or six short pieces of tying thread
Back: Deer body hair pulled forward over body
Head: Trimmed back hair butts

Jassid. Vince Marinaro's famous fly has become one of the most important artificials in the angler's book. When small beetles and leafhoppers
are on the water, I would not want to be without a copy.

Hook: Size 20 to 22
Thread: Black
Body: Black hackle tied palmer, trimmed top and bottom
Wings: Jungle cock nail, set flat

Letort Crickets and Hoppers. When the summer months arrive, it means that most of the significant mayfly hatches are over; it also means that the crickets and hoppers have fully developed kickers and the meadows are full of life. The two best imitations for this new "hatch" are the Letort Cricket and the Letort Hopper, both designed by one of America's finest trout anglers, Ed Shenk, of Pennylvania.

LETORT CRICKET

Hook: Size 10 to 14
Thread: Black
Body: Black fur dubbing
Wings: Black quill section set flat, dyed black deer body hair over
Head: Hair from wing butts trimmed

LETORT HOPPER

Hook: Size 8 to 12
Thread: Yellow
Body: Yellowish-tan fur dubbing
Wings: Brown mottled turkey quill section, set flat; natural deer body
          hair over
Head: Hair from wing butts trimmed

Terrestrials: A. *Ant.* B. *Jassid.* C. *Letort Hopper.*

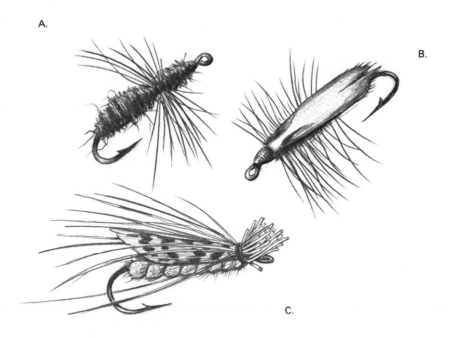

A.

B.

C.

My Favorite Places to Fish	Type of Fish	Best Time	Suggested Flies Type	Size
Letort, Carlisle, Pennsylvania	Brown	Spring and summer	1. Cressbug 2. Black Beetle 3. Hopper	16 14–16 10–12
Falling Spring Creek, Chambersburg, Pennsylvania	Brown Rainbow Brook	Spring and summer	1. Caenis 2. Cricket 3. Sulphur Dun	24–28 14 14–16

Beaverkill, Roscoe, New York	Brown Rainbow	Spring and fall	1. Caddis
			2. Gray Fox
			    Variant
			3. Large Dun
			    Variant
				10–16
				
				8–10
				
				10

Main Delaware River, New York	Rainbow Brown	May–June September–October	1. Brown Drake
			2. March Brown
			3. Gray, Royal,
			    and White
			    Wulffs
				10–14
				10–14
				
				8–16

McKenzie River, Oregon	Brook Brown Rainbow	Spring and fall	1. Caddis 2. Humpy 3. Adams 4. White Wulff	8–16 8–16 10–20 8–14

A. *Letort Cricket.*
B. *Cutwing parachute dun.*
C. *Beetle.*

Since 1934 Charles F. Waterman has written outdoor material. Wintering in Florida and then moving to Montana for the summer and fall, he still travels whenever possible—to Alaska, to Argentina, to Canada—always seeking to broaden his knowledge of hunting and fishing.

He is a newspaper and magazine columnist and is the author of eight books on hunting and fishing: The Hunter's World, The Fisherman's World, Hunting in America, Fishing in America, Modern Fresh and Salt Water Fly Fishing, The Part I Remember, Hunting Upland Birds, *and a new, as yet untitled book on trout fishing.*

5. Tackle for Fishing the Dry Fly
Rods, Reels, Lines
Leaders, and Knots

Charles F. Waterman

THERE ARE STREAMS where a carefully selected willow switch will work just as well as a $300 split-bamboo rod, but dry-fly fishermen are perfectionists, lovers of fine things, and frequently traditionalists.

These facts are dramatized by a man kneeling beside a brook he could jump across and dapping a size 20 fly with only the leader extended from the tip. Although he might fish thusly for most of the day, he would preach endlessly about the merits of his Leonard rod and his English reel. The meanest thing to be said on the subject is that some connoisseurs of fine fly tackle could not tell the difference between a mass-produced factory cull and the finest hand-laminated cane without trademarks and outward appearance. And some anglers who have not learned to do more than flop cast would have no flies except those tied by recognized masters of the art.

So you can say that much fine tackle is wasted on the inept—but then there are drivers who can hardly get out of a supermarket parking lot but who feel a burning need for a Porsche or BMW.

Tackle recommendations tend to be general, for we all know that lines, leaders, and rods must be matched to their users as well as to each other. No two casters operate exactly alike, even on the same streams, and most of us have tried some wretched combinations (for us) that came to vibrant life in the hands of the masters who loved them. Nothing is perfect for everybody, but we'll stick to observations that we fondly believe to be factual and possibly helpful to lost souls among the willows and the slippery rocks.

67

RODS

The rod is the big item for an average fly fisherman, and he proudly considers it the most valuable piece of fishing equipment that he uses. A startling inventory of his fly boxes, however, might reveal that he's actually invested more in hair and feathers than in bamboo, glass, or graphite. Some popular opinions about rods may be completely false but they persist because they once had basis in fact. We'll study the rods first.

For a long time there was a big thing about wet-fly rods and dry-fly rods, but that's largely ignored today simply because the soft and weepy action of the wet-fly rod doesn't often show up any more. Rods have a crisper action than they used to have. Thirty years ago a rod builder told me: "Hell, the old wet-fly action was a carry-over from bait fishing. These new ones do just as well with a wet and a lot better with a dry."

The actual weight of rods doesn't mean much any more. Weights of the most delicate bamboos lost much of their gee-whiz effect when glass appeared in lighter form; then graphite came along and smeared the whole works by being still lighter and often much stiffer.

Rod materials? There is no best material, but I will do some classifying—in general—losing friends and infuriating strangers.

So far, I tend toward bamboo rods that take light lines up to about No. 6, being partial to the vaunted "bamboo feel," which nobody seems able to describe. Light bamboos tend toward delicacy and are somewhat forgiving of sloppy casting (most bamboo-lovers won't admit that), and their weight is not hard on the physique. When you get to a rod that takes a No. 7 line (that's getting fairly heavy for trout but has a definite place with some big dries), I part company with bamboo and go for glass or graphite. I'm afraid the big bamboo salmon rod that takes a No. 10 line and weighs 7 or 8 ounces has had it with me. Although some distance casters use the bamboo in tournaments, the typical cane fishing rod won't stay in there with glass or graphite with all that line out; it weighs too much.

Glass has been around long enough that almost any action can be built into it, and if somebody says that he "can't fish with glass," chances are he hasn't tried enough rods.

Graphite rods have had breakage problems, but they seem to be on the wane. I have two graphites that have been through the mill since the material first became available. Most graphites are fairly stiff, and without running through a lot of stress and strain stuff that neither of us understands, let's just say that they bend about so far and then stiffen up suddenly, whereas glass or bamboo has more follow-through. That's a generality, but it's pretty close.

Perfect dry-fly water in a spring-fed creek where the constant flow permits shoals of vegetation. Such streams are extremely fertile, with very high populations of insects.

I have found it easier to make a fairly long cast with a graphite rod than with glass. When extreme range is reached, I find there isn't much difference in good rods taking the same kind of line; but then we get into the individual stick, and the longest thrower (by not far) I own happens to be graphite. Then I drop down to a glass rod that shades a graphite using the same weight line. In the future there will be more variety in graphite action.

From the 12-foot trout rods of one hundred years ago, we went shorter and lighter until a short rod became a mark of an expert; we eventually got down to some 6-footers and less. In 90 percent of fishing that's too short. If you have only one dry-fly rod and are without prejudice, make it 7½ to 8 feet long. Until about 1970 the trend was to shorter rods, and 7 feet was average for light dry-fly operations. Sticks are getting longer now. I grudgingly admit that a 10½-foot graphite I used recently is a marvel for holding line up over the rough water and getting a long float with a dry. I spent last summer with an 8-footer for the most part, but there are exceptional cases. Over open water the only advantage of a short rod is its low profile from the trout's viewpoint.

The other day I found myself stuck in a narrow North Carolina

Landing dry-fly trout from a western freestone creek.

creek with brush and overhanging trees and reverted to the 6½-foot
bamboo I once bought to prove what a hell-slather fisherman I was.
Making sidearm casts almost parallel to the water, it was a marvel—the
perfect choice for short casts in limited space. Then on a Pennsylvania
limestone creek (see what a world traveler I am?) I went to an 8-foot
bamboo instead of the 8-foot graphite I had been using for dry flies.

Now came something strange, for although I *believe* the slower
bamboo gave me a more delicate cast, I found it was hard to dry the fly
in the air. With the graphite, a little flick almost popped the fly, making
it give a little plip up there in the air and showering moisture (you know
the feel) without snapping it off. The bamboo didn't want to dry my fly
for me without special effort, but the casting motion was more fluid.

Such remarks won't select rods for you, but they may make you
think about it more.

Almost all dry-fly fishing for trout, salmon, smallmouth bass, and
panfish can be handled beautifully with two rods. Have one that takes a
line from No. 4 to No. 6 and is 7 to 8 feet long. Then get one that takes
a No. 8 and is about 8½ feet long. The latter will work on bugs if they
aren't too large and will slam big bushy things into the wind, as on
salmon streams, smallmouth rivers, and places where big trout are taking hoppers or stone flies a long way off.

If you want a third rod, maybe that little short rig will be worth-
while for narrow brushy creeks, when you wade up the middle or close
to the left bank. There are other waters where a long rod will keep the
line *above* streamside brush, will hold more line off the water, and can
be better used for dapping into impossible spots—a business you must
see at work before you fully appreciate it.

Rod grips are a matter of personal taste, and although a hammer-
handle shape is one of the most comfortable (oval in cross section), you'll
see few of them, because they take handwork instead of simple turning.
In efficiency, it's no big thing. A flattened area for your thumb may help
a little. I can't say I've ever used a really troublesome rod handle, except in a case where the grip of an extremely powerful rod was too small
and needed building up.

When it comes to reel seats, I have livid complaints about the ones
with simple sliding rings over cork and no locking feature. They look
dainty on a small rod and less hardware makes for less weight, but the
people who build my reels don't seem to make them to stay on those
fickle, friction-tight Tinker Toys. Unless I resort to plastic tape, I spend
considerable time groping for my reel in cold water. A pox upon the
design.

Until recently there was no contest about guides for light fly rods. Now the light "speed ring" type of aluminum oxide comes on as a competitor of plain wire snake guides. I have a rod that is completely equipped with them, and it casts beautifully although a mite heavier than with plain wire. They're great as stripping guides and as tip-tops, but their merit on the rest of the shaft is seldom noticeable in moderate casting.

Most wiggling, whipping, and flailing tests of fly rods as carried on by shoppers in tackle stores don't mean much, and few fishermen know what they have until a line is fitted and they really start casting. The fact is that tackle counter testing is one instance where the actual scale weight of the rod, especially the tip, makes a great deal of difference in its performance. With a bamboo rod, for example, some of the tip weight takes the place of line weight in testing wiggles. With a light graphite stick, the tip doesn't flap much in unlined waving because it doesn't weigh enough. I have known fishermen to report immediately that a graphite rod (unlined) was too stiff for any kind of use.

You can tell the pattern of a rod's bend, however, without putting a line on it. Put the tip against the floor or wall and press gently, or make a casting motion and note whether the rod bends mostly at the tip, through its entire length, or in a graduated manner. The "flippy tip" rods of a few years ago have mercifully faded from the scene; the full parabolic action isn't around much either. Most rods for dry-fly fishing bend increasingly toward the tip, and they tend to be so similar in action that the only way to learn their differences is to compare several at the same time.

LINES

The traditional line for trout fishing is the double taper, slenderized at each end and with a long, heavy section in between. You can fish successfully forever with no other type. It's actually two lines in one; for if one end shows wear, reverse the whole thing and start over.

The tapered tip and level belly make it possible to deliver a fly with more delicacy than is possible with a level line or with a weight-forward line at normal casting distances. Most dry-fly angling does not involve casts of more than forty feet. Generally, dragfree floats are difficult to manage farther than that, but there are a thousand exceptions.

Of late the weight-forward line is used more and more, even with dry flies, simply because it gives more distance, but some of the principles involved are poorly understood. You can false cast much more of the double taper or even the level. Distance with the weight-forward

Placid spring creeks such as this one offer some of the more difficult trout fishing but often have large populations of fish.

line is achieved because of the relatively light running line toward the rear that carries easily as the heavy forward section is thrown. This light running material will not carry up if you try to false cast too long a line. For example, if the heavy belly section of a weight-forward line is thirty feet long, false cast only a little more than that and shoot for distance. When you shoot much line, you cannot achieve as soft a presentation. The ultrasmooth turnover of the double taper is supported by the heavy section running clear back to the rod.

I made a fool of myself on an Atlantic salmon stream several years ago by using a weight-forward line with a short head alongside fishermen with double tapers. The fish were close enough that they could be reached easily with the double taper but far enough that I had to shoot considerable line with my weight-forward, and try as I would I could not get the proper action with my fly; it simply didn't alight with the leader properly straight. By the time I had things working right, my feathers had passed the fish which my neighbors were catching with regularity.

There are places, however, where the weight-forward is a help, generally when the river is wide and the fly big. It has no proper place on small streams.

If all your casts are to be quite short, you'll probably do better with a well-loaded or even overloaded rod—the exact opposite of the popular theory that "you don't need a heavy line for short casts." In other words, if the cast is fairly long and a No. 5 line carries enough weight to make the rod work properly, you might need a No. 6 to make the rod work well at very short distances where you don't have much line out.

A good example of this shows up in fishing dry flies from a boat drifting close to a shore where the fish are living. With a light line the casting becomes hard work. With a short section of heavy line out the rod works as it would with a longer light line, and the arm and wrist action is moderate. Ideally, you can do away with false casting completely unless it is needed to dry a fly.

A high-floating line will pick up a dry fly with less disturbance than will a soggy one, and although they'll tell you modern fly lines will float without dressing, frequent doses of cleaner will make them work better. Floating covers a multitude of performances, and some waters carry materials that will make a line groggy in short order.

I am romantically inclined toward light-colored or brilliant lines; I love to watch them slide through the air and form graceful loops. But there are cases where a dark or dull-colored line is less likely to scare spooky fish. Green and brown are decidedly less visible, but if you are having casting troubles, something brighter will show you what is happening with less squinting.

Let's admit that there are many cases when you can't see your dry fly because of poor light conditions, because the fly is very small, or because the current is too rough. In such cases you look for the splash of a fish's rise, but they don't always splash. A twitch of a highly visible line has saved many a strike for me, even though such things are generally associated with underwater nymphs. Many top fishermen use indicators of one kind or another at the tips of their lines, and the Cortland people have a line with a slightly enlarged bright orange tip, primarily for nymph fishing, but in many instances it is good with dries.

There are sinking lines and wet-tip lines that have proved invaluable for other fishing. I have never found any use for them in dry-fly operations.

REELS

Traditional fly reels are single action. There is too much fuss made about matching light reels to light rods, and if you must nibble at that, hypothetically the ideal combination would have the rod balancing exactly where you hold it. A heavy reel is a help in saving energy on a heavy rod. Admittedly, you get a more lively feel and perhaps added sensitivity if a rod is slightly tip heavy as you hold it, quite practical in light trout sticks.

The disadvantages of tiny reels are that it requires a lot of cranking to take up much line and that when your line and leader have been stored on a small spool, they come off in loops. The leader is harder to straighten, and the line will be a minor nuisance if you make a long cast and find a corkscrew bumping through the guides.

Very little dry-fly fishing requires more drag than is needed to keep the reel from overrunning as you strip line from it. With a fish on, the bend of the rod provides a great deal of drag automatically, and it can be instantly reduced or increased by raising or lowering the tip. If you're dealing with large fish, there are precision reels with fine drags that will work on salmon, steelhead, and saltwater fish. They are expensive and heavy, and if I knew a fish would weigh 50 pounds, I'd prefer one—but many fish of more than 100 pounds have been landed with reels having minimal drags.

Multiplying reels have the advantage of saving time when you have a great deal of line out, which is more important in heavy fishing. Automatic reels, generally in disfavor with traditionalists, don't work on fish that make long runs, don't hold a great deal of line, and are heavy. They do save your line from considerable abuse, always keeping it out from underfoot with a touch of your finger.

Costly imported reels, generally British, usually contain workmanship justifying their price but may be less durable than less expensive ones.

If you must be completely practical, have duplicate reels with extra spools that can be installed easily. It can be bad news if a fine, lightweight reel is dropped hard enough to bend the frame. Straightening a fly reel frame can be an engineering feat, especially if the tolerances are expensively small. A sloppy fit may be better. Honest.

For ultralight weight with respectable size, I like a reel that is made mostly of graphite.

Right- or left-hand wind? That's easily summarized, and we'll suppose the fisherman to be right-handed. If he winds with his left hand, he can leave his right hand on the rod grip. Some anglers, however, feel it's nice to change hands occasionally to rest the casting hand. The left-hand wind leaves your more dexterous and stronger fist to handle the rod while playing a fish. But most of us can wind much faster with our right hand, and that can be mighty helpful when a fish rushes at your waders. I used the left-hand wind for twenty-five years and have now

William Downey fishes from an artificial "path" on Pennsylvania's Letort, some of the most delicate of limestone water.

used the right-hand wind for twenty-five. I haven't decided yet for certain which turns out better.

LEADERS

I consider any leader to be long if it's more than 12 feet. Most fish are caught on leaders that are a little longer than the rod, but in some situations of spooky fish, clear, calm water, and little wind, you might go to 20 feet. I doubt if much is gained after the first 15, for if the 20-footer casts well, it will be tapered to a heavy butt section that will hit the water almost as hard as the tip of the line.

Most veterans tie up their own tapered leaders, and excellent formulas for that can be found. The blood knots holding the sections together don't seem to scare fish and may actually help the leader turn over. Many fishermen attach a butt section to the line and leave it there for a season or two, changing the rest of the leader to suit conditions. And many use knotless tapered leaders for most of the length and simply add the tippet called for.

Almost all leaders are monofilament these days. A few folks cling to silkworm gut, but it's expensive, hard to find, and has the same disadvantages that it had when we gleefully reached for the new nylon. The majority of fishermen like stiff nylon for the butt section but may go for limp material for the tippet. I don't think the stiff or limp business is too important unless we deal with extremes. A stiff butt section helps straighten the cast but tends to be kinky as it comes off a reel or storage spool. A limp tippet is more likely to tangle but often gives you a few extra inches of dragfree float, because it curls with the current as the fly drifts.

Leader color doesn't excite me much, and the fact is that the most deceptive shade depends upon the background the fish sees it against—sky, brush, stone, or broken current. Move the sun or the clouds and all of that can change.

Tippet size can be much smaller when using strong monofilament than it was when we used treacherous gut. It is measured from 0X, which measures .011 inch, on down to 7X (.004 inch) and smaller. Strength varies with the material, but let's say a 5X tippet will test about 2½ pounds and is probably the most popular size for light dry-fly fishing. Most of us have to be careful with 6X and tend to break off fish with 7X, even though it is occasionally necessary.

It's a bitter truth that a master fisherman (who could handle the smallest leader better than an amateur) can get by with a bigger tippet than less skillful operators. I sadly remember a fisherman who could catch fish on 5X without difficulty, while I was forced to 6X simply because he presented the fly better and made less fuss with his larger tippet.

In addition to less visibility, the light tippet allows the small fly to perform better. If you're using a size 20 (that's pretty small change), you'll probably need a 6X tippet to make it float right. Hook sizes are inconsistent, and there are fishermen who take great pride in very small stuff; sometimes their "24" is as large as somebody else's "20." And the fly itself is pretty hard to describe by hook size alone.

Some fishermen in certain instances place great store in making their leaders sink near the fly, and others actually dope their leaders to make them float. There's a theory that a trout can see the leader anyway if he looks at it, and that a trout that takes is satisfactorily distracted from the leader.

With small flies and near-surface nymphs an indicator on the leader is frequently helpful. Harry Murray, a Virginia angler who may be seen in the West as well as on Pennsylvania limestone waters, threads on a bit of bright orange fly line well down the leader. I've used little dabs of fluorescent yarn cemented to a knot or tied in with it. If such dinguses scare the fish, I've seen no proof of it.

KNOTS

The dry-fly user needs few, but good, knots. The improved clinch is excellent for attaching fly to leader. The blood knot is accepted as best for making up the leader sections. A nail knot is hard to beat for attaching leader to line and is sometimes refined with the use of a needle so that the leader comes out of the line's center rather than from its side. Line-to-backing is generally handled with the nail knot, and the addition of Pliobond or other cement to the nail knots will make them smoother. These are good essential ties and should be done carefully.

My Favorite Places to Fish	Type of Fish	Best Time	Suggested Flies Type	Size
Armstrong Spring Creek, Livingston, Montana	Rainbow Brown	August– October	1. Light Cahill 2. Adams 3. Blue Dun	16–20 16–20 18–20
Smith River, White Sulphur Springs, Montana	Rainbow Brown Cutthroat Brook	July–August	1. Royal Wulff 2. Joe's Hopper 3. Goofus Bug	10–14 10 10–12
Slough Creek, Yellowstone National Park, Wyoming	Rainbow Cutthroat	July–August	1. Goofus Bug 2. Joe's Hopper 3. Trude	12 10 12
Sebago Lakes, Maine	Smallmouth	June	1. Powderpuff 2. Sofa Pillow	1/0 1/0
Mills River, Pisgah National Forest, North Carolina	Rainbow Brown Brook	May	1. Light Cahill 2. Blue Dun 3. Adams	16 16 14

Improved Clinch Knot

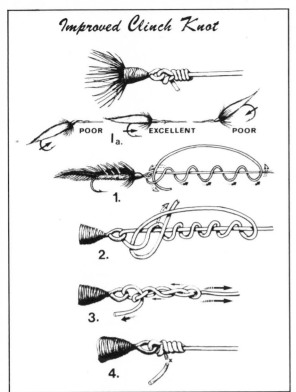

POOR   EXCELLENT   POOR

1a.

1.

2.

3.

4.

Blood Knot

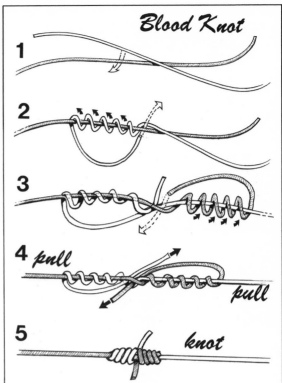

1

2

3

4 pull   pull

5 knot

Nail (tube) Knot

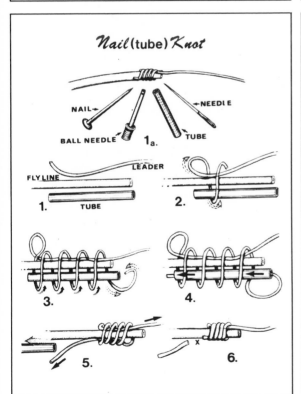

NAIL   NEEDLE
BALL NEEDLE   1a.   TUBE

FLY LINE   LEADER
1.   TUBE

2.

3.

4.

5.

6.

Improved Turle Knot

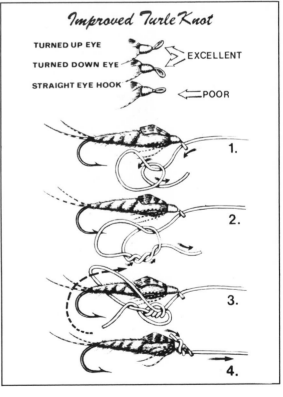

TURNED UP EYE
TURNED DOWN EYE   EXCELLENT
STRAIGHT EYE HOOK   POOR

1.

2.

3.

4.

Bernard "Lefty" Kreh is a member of the Fishing Hall of Fame. He has fished in all the Canadian provinces, in Alaska, and in many other parts of the world.

He is on the advisory board of the American League of Anglers, the Federation of Fly Fishermen, and the Salt Water Fly Rodders of America. He is a casting instructor and a consultant in the design of fishing tackle.

He is nationally known as a flytier and lecturer and has been an outdoor writer for more than twenty years. His most recent book is Fly Casting with Lefty Kreh.

6. Casting a Dry Fly
Fundamentals, Curves, the Roll, and Double Haul

Bernard "Lefty" Kreh

CASTING A DRY FLY boils down to a matter of putting it on the water so that it doesn't startle the fish and so that it will float in a manner that appears natural. Between the backcast and the final float, a few rules must be learned—not too complicated, but necessary.

Good fly casting starts with a proper pickup of the line and fly. Most dry-fly fishermen do it wrong, and, like everything else, if you get off to a bad start, it spoils the performance.

Certainly one of the most common casting faults is that the angler starts with the rod too high. Realize that the line is slack, the rod is straight and unloaded, and you want to throw the line behind you—not *down* and behind you. A rod held at 60 degrees from the surface (as many fishermen do) at the beginning of the cast must lift all the line from the water, get loaded, then make the power stroke. At the moment the rod is loaded with a taut line free of the surface, the angle of power thrust must of necessity be down and behind, since the rod tip has traveled so far back of the fisherman.

Proper technique requires that the angler lower the rod tip, pointing it toward the fly. Remove the slack with your other hand. The fly will never move until all slack has been taken from the line—a vital point in any kind of fly casting. Once the slack is gone, bring the rod smoothly but swiftly up until the rod hand is about head level, then (with no pause or break in the lift) make the power snap in the direction you want the line to go. Few anglers understand that it is the *direction of the power snap that determines where the line will go*—nothing else!

If the rod has been lowered and you make a good lift, you have the ability to make a backcast in any direction you care from a towering steeple cast to a very low one. But if you start with a high rod, you are committed to a low and probably sloppy backcast.

Of vital importance in dry-fly fishing is the ability to control the size of your loop. As the line unrolls behind and in front it forms a loop. For economy a tight loop is best. This develops less air resistance and requires less energy to hold the loop upright as it unrolls.

For many dry-fly situations, however, a wide loop is more desirable. A tight loop travels at a high speed and can cause you to overcast, driving the fly into the water. When a truly delicate cast is called for, most anglers will do better to use a wide loop. Such a loop tends to die as it reaches the target, and as the line slows down reduced energy causes the fly to come over and alight gently.

Of course, much casting is into small pockets and sometimes into the breeze. So, like all other types of fly casting, it is vital to be able to throw the size loop that you want for specific fishing situations.

Loop size is directly related to the length of the power stroke. To be sure that we understand the power stroke, this is the quick thrust made to propel the fly behind or in front of us. The follow-through and arm movements are separate events.

A short power stroke will develop a tight small loop, a long power stroke a bigger loop, and a very long stroke will give you a huge loop. There are times when you want to make an incredibly short power stroke to toss a tight loop into the breeze or through a hole in the brush. At other times a gentle delivery of the fly on placid waters will require that you make a longish power snap to get the desired results.

Earlier I said that the direction of the power stroke determines the direction that the line loop will travel. One of the most common faults is the leader's banging against the line at the end of the cast, resulting in a poor presentation—or worse, a knot in the tippet.

With two exceptions that I know about, all tangles in leaders at the end of the cast come from a cast that is brought straight back, then straight forward. Let's use a living room floor to explain what I mean. If you were to lay five feet of fly line on the floor, move it backwards its full length, then come forward on the exact plane, it is obvious that the line is going to run together. The same thing will happen when you throw the line behind you and come forward on the same plane. If the power snap back and the power snap forward are exactly opposite to each other (180 degrees), then the two casts must run into each other.

Tangled leaders also result from a cast that is made too soon, with the rod overhead. What happens is that the stroke is perfectly parallel with the water, and the line is being directed straight ahead and will again run into itself. Often when you make this cast the line will strike the tip top of the rod—an indication that the power stroke has been made too soon.

Another way of getting leader tangles is to bring the elbow and arm straight back and straight forward, sending the line behind and forward on the same plane (as on the floor); they are surely going to run into each other.

We often have read of the high backcast. In fact, many anglers teach that you should throw the high backcast most of the time. That's wrong! The rule governing backcast should be: *Throw the lowest back-cast you can for existing fishing conditions*. The higher you throw the backcast, the more problems you build for yourself. It is almost impossible to throw a truly high backcast and throw a forward cast where the leader doesn't come down and strike the line. The lower the cast is made, the easier it is to keep the casting planes separated and the loop under control. In my judgment, a good tight-loop forward cast is made with a low backcast that passes so close to the tip on the forward power stroke that it almost touches it.

On the forward cast the greatest fault of most casters who have finally learned to throw the size loop they want is that they lower their rod too quickly after the forward power stroke. This pulls the base of the loop away from the top and destroys the configuration of the loop. You must wait until the loop is a short distance in front of you before lowering the rod; this keeps the rod tip far enough away so that it can't affect the loop size.

Once these techniques are mastered, you must be able to make a slack-line cast for proper presentation to many fish. A line that falls straight on the water will be acted upon by various currents and will create drag that pulls the fly around unnaturally, causing the trout to refuse it. If slack is thrown into the cast, the slack must be washed out before you get drag effects.

One of the best techniques is simply to cast hard and high above the target, stopping the rod quickly at the end of the power stroke. It's important to keep the rod held high. As the line speeds through the air, it comes tight against the vertical rod and snaps back, the forward end falling in folds on the water. At this point lower the rear of the rod to add additional slack farther back in the line. The line will float along in loose waves, allowing a float for a relatively long distance before the currents cause the dry fly to drag. It takes a little practice to get the accuracy needed, but this is perhaps the simplest method of getting slack into a cast.

Left and right curves are used by all experienced anglers who float dry flies to shy trout. This simply means that the line and leader curve to the left or to the right from the angler, allowing the fly to float down to the fish *before* the leader and line. Often this is the only way to take shy trout; it is a technique that is vital to good dry-fly work.

I began to experiment around 1970 while fishing on the Cane River in North Carolina as a guest of Hugh Chatham. This great stream, private water, has many large trout that are wise in the ways of fishermen. I wanted to be able to make curves to the left and to the right, but in many places the stream is so narrow that I had difficulty making the side cast, which is used by most anglers to get a curve in the line. I knew that the line goes in the direction of the power stroke, so I began fooling around and developed what for me is a different, far easier, and much more accurate method of making a curve to the left or to the right.

Remember only one thing and you can soon practice and perfect this cast: Wherever the power snap or stroke goes, the line will go.

Let's assume you want to make a curve to the right—the one that most anglers have problems with. Throw a normal backcast, come forward as you always have, but make the power stroke by snapping sharply forward, making a right-angle (90-degree) turn in the snap, so that at the end of the power stroke the thumb (on top of the rod handle) is pointing to the right. A little practice will allow you to direct the cast so that you can make the fly land where you want it to.

For a left-hand curve, simply come forward and power snap the stroke in a left 90-degree angle.

There are several advantages to this technique. Many small streams have overhead casting room but not side room; this technique takes care of that.

Second, the accuracy you get with this cast is amazing.

Third, it is much easier to learn than the other method. Most fishermen can throw a fair curve to the left but have all kinds of trouble with one to the right.

Something should be said about the presentation of a dry fly to a trout. One of the best methods of delivering a fly is to be at a downstream point that is at a 45-degree angle from the fish and make a slack-line cast. This is the way most beginners deliver the fly.

What you never do is drop a fly line or leader on the surface directly over a trout. For that reason it is usually poor technique to fish directly downstream of a fish.

Should you make a poor cast, don't jerk it out. Almost always it is best to allow the line to float well downcurrent of the fish so that a silent pickup can be made.

Double hauling is a technique developed for tournament casting that has been applied to almost every phase of fishing. It is important to know what double hauling actually does. *Double hauling only increases line speed—nothing else!* It does not make you a better caster. In fact, it only results in the average fly fisherman throwing his casting mistakes over a longer distance faster! Good rod-hand technique is more important.

To double haul, the angler, using his right hand on the rod, will jerk the line sharply downward with his left hand as the power snap is made. This radically increases line speed. If the two hands were approximately ten inches apart at the beginning of the backcast, the left hand should come back to within ten inches of the rod hand at the end of the backcast. The two hands travel forward as the rod is loaded. When the forward power snap is made, the left hand again makes a short, sharp downward pull on the line, adding velocity.

Basic faults in double hauling are too much force and too long a stroke. A good double hauler stores the left hand's energy until the precise moment that he is going to make the power snap. Then he makes both power moves together. The left hand only needs to move in the snap a few inches, whereas most anglers jerk down a foot or more, destroying the effectiveness of double hauling.

Double hauling has limited use in dry-fly work but can be a lifesaver at times.

For about 50 or more percent of our casts most of us make a single haul. As the rod is lifted for the backcast, make a little tug with the left hand, adding efficiency to the cast. Occasionally, you'll make a poor forward cast that tends to die toward the end, and a simple single haul can pick up the line speed enough to turn the fly over properly.

Roll casting has much use in dry-fly work. Again, most people don't understand the single important factor in roll casting. Roll casting is a method of flipping the line in front of you without the aid of a backcast. If you have ever tried to roll cast on a lawn or gym floor, you know it can't be done well. That is because the line needs some resistance on it so that the rod can be loaded to make the cast. A slick gym floor or grass causes the line to continually move toward the angler, and the rod can never be properly loaded. This is an extremely important point missed by many anglers who have been roll casting for years.

To get the rod properly loaded, you must cause the line to stop or to come as near as possible to a dead stop on the water. Surface tension grips the line and the more the line is stopped, the more of an increase there is in resistance, allowing the rod to properly load.

Three steps will allow anyone to roll cast well in minutes: Bring the rod back slowly; stop the line; make a sharp snap like a hammerblow in the direction you want the fly to go.

LIFTING THE FLY FROM THE WATER

First remove all slack from line as rod tip is lowered so it points toward the fly.

Begin swiftly, but smoothly, to raise the rod tip. This starts removing the line from the water.

Without pausing, continue to raise the rod quickly. Note that most of the line is now free of the surface.

When nothing but a foot or two of fly line, or just the leader, is on the surface, make the short power stroke to form the desired loop. Please note carefully that the rod is almost vertical, not lying back, as the power stroke begins.

Because all or nearly all of the fly line was removed from the surface before the backcast was made, almost no effort is needed for the power stroke, and the rod and line remain free of shock waves.

CASTING PROBLEMS AND FAULTS

This photo shows a fairly tight loop, one that drives well into the breeze or can be utilized to throw a long distance or into a tight spot.

A wide loop is illustrated here. This tends to die near the end of its flight, giving you a delicate presentation on flat waters.

Paul Brunn, Jr., Jackson Hole fishing guide and outdoor writer, demonstrates what happens to the backcast if the rod is held too high at the start of the cast. Before the rod and line are off the water and in flight, the rod has been carried so far back that the rod tip has formed slack. This slack in the line must be removed on the forward stroke before the rod will begin to bring the fly forward.

Here Paul has formed a good tight loop that should send the line swiftly over the water.

But by dropping the tip (a common fault among casters), Paul destroyed the loop configuration when he pulled the base away from the top.

Some casters make the power stroke too soon. When this happens, the fly or leader runs into the tip top of the rod as is about to occur here.

Making the stroke high overhead, so that the rod tip moves parallel to the water, will cause the loop to run into itself.

Bringing the elbow straight back and straight forward will keep the back and forward casts on the same plane, and again they will run into each other, as shown. This is called a tailing loop.

Sometimes from the same fault as in the preceding photo you will get the disastrous results shown here.

Making your power strokes straight back and straight forward can produce a tailing loop or cause the leader or line to run together.

When a very high backcast is made, a tailing loop almost always occurs. It is extremely difficult to throw the line way overhead and then not strike the leader and fly on the forward portion of the line as you deliver the fly. It can be done, but this cast requires a lot of practice and should be mastered for those situations that require it.

SLACK LINE CAST FOR DRAG-FREE DRIFT

A high cast with excessive speed is made over the target area. It is important not to lower the rod but to keep it high and nearly vertical. The line will completely extend and come tight against the rod, causing it to bend and then recover, and jarring the rod so the line at the leader end falls in a number of loose waves on the surface.

As soon as the forward portion falls to the water, lower the rod to create additional slack nearer the angler. This will give you slack throughout the cast as shown.

CURVE CASTS

Curve casts are explained in the text. The method I use does not require the rod to be brought forward to the side, as in the conventional manner, but with the rod almost vertical, as shown.

To make a curve to the left, simply make a power stroke that curves sharply to the left throughout the stroke and the curve will fall as shown. The vital point to remember is that wherever the power stroke goes, the line will go.

Here the angler has come forward vertically and made a power snap to the right. To add even more curve you can drop the rod tip away as shown.

Results of a curve to the right.

MISTAKES IN PRESENTING A FLY

The most serious mistake you can make in dry-fly casting is to drop the line and fly over the fish, as shown with this white model of a trout. The line splash on the water will surely put down any wise trout.

Here the angler has made a good downstream approach and thrown the proper curve to the left. But the fly, shown in the white circle, is well to the left of the trout, which will not see it. Curve casts, or any other casts to a trout, must come nearly over the head of the fish as the fly drifts with the current. This cast is useless, but the wise angler, to avoid alarming the trout, will allow the fly to drift far below the fish before lifting it from the surface.

Here the angler has made a curve to the right, but even though the fly is nearer the trout, it probably isn't close enough to be seen or to interest the fish in chasing it.

THE ROLL CAST

Begin the roll cast by sliding the line slowly toward you, or picking up slack as the fly drifts down-current to you.

Continue to slide the line back slowly (this is very important) as the rod tip is raised.

When the line falls behind you, as the arrow shows, allow the line to come as close to a full stop on the water as possible.

Use the same quick sharp snap of the wrist to make a power stroke as you would in a tight-loop long-distance cast. Note that the rod is stopped high and the line comes forward unrolling.

The line unrolls completely as the fly turns over on target. If the thumb is on top of the rod, the snap will direct the cast in the direction in which the thumb is pointed, and great accuracy results. If the fly falls in a tangle of line short of the target, you made your power stroke angled too far down in front of you. Should the line rise up in the air and fall short, you directed the power stroke too high.

THE ROLL CAST SEEN FROM THE FRONT

These front views of a roll cast show that the rod tip is held away from the body slightly, to keep the line from falling against the rod, and give a fuller idea of rod angles and line work.

THE SIDE ROLL CAST

A cast that allows the line to unroll and stay near the water, barely missing it, will often enable the fisherman to set a fly down under overhanging branches. The side roll cast is especially valuable for such work. It is made in almost the same manner as a conventional roll cast. This photo shows the line after it has been slid on the water, has fallen behind the back of the angler, and has been allowed to pause.

As the forward cast is started, the rod is dropped down until it is almost parallel to the water.

Immediately, the power snap is made parallel to the water.

Line and fly begin to unroll in a plane parallel to the surface.

At the end of the cast the line has straightened; at no point did the line rise more than two feet above the water.

| My Favorite Places to Fish | Type of Fish | Best Time | Suggested Flies | |
			Type	Size
Streams of western North Carolina	Brook Brown Rainbow	Early summer	1. Spirit 2. Adams 3. Light Cahill	12–14 12–14 12–14
Yellowstone Park	Cutthroat Brook Brown Rainbow	Late summer– early fall	1. Humpy 2. Adams 3. Hopper	12–16 12–18 4, 6, 10
Henrys Fork and Snake River, Idaho	Brook Brown Rainbow	Early fall	1. Light Olive 2. Adams 3. Light Cahill	16–20 12, 16, 20 12–18
Letort and Falling Springs	Brook Brown	August– September	1. Letort, Cricket 2. Beetle 3. Ant	10 12–16 12, 16, 20
Snake River, Jackson Hole area, Idaho	Brown Cutthroat Rainbow	September	1. Humpy 2. Hopper 3. Adams	10, 12, 16 6–10 12, 16, 18

Len Wright has been a compulsive fisherman ever since he could wade. After graduating from Harvard he served as a fighter pilot in World War II and then worked in the Pentagon as a desk chief in the military intelligence service. From an advertising agency background, he joined The New York Times *as an executive.*

He lives in New York City but has a weekend home overlooking a famous Catskill trout stream. As a member of the American League of Anglers, the Theodore Gordon Flyfishers, and the Angler's Club of New York, he works for conservation.

His articles on fishing have appeared in The New York Times Magazine, Esquire, Signature, Field & Stream, Sports Afield, The Fly Fisherman, Gray's Sporting Journal, *and many other periodicals.*

He is the author of Fishing the Dry Fly as a Living Insect *and* Fly-fishing Heresies.

7. The Water and the Fish
Rise Forms, Clues, and Imitations

Leonard M. Wright, Jr.

NO OTHER FORM of freshwater fishing is as considered or deliberate as dry-fly fishing. When conditions for the floating fly are perfect, each presentation can put your fly over the precise position of a fish you know is taking food from the surface. Perhaps this is one of the main charms of the game: There's little random searching or prospecting. When fish are rising steadily, it can be all play and no work.

Because this type of fishing is so visual, your approach to the water you are about to cover should be watchful and deliberate. If you step right in and start casting the moment your tackle is rigged up, you will be limiting not only your own savoring of the sport, but your chances of success as well. Whether you're fishing a lake, a pond, a stream, or a river, the minutes spent observing before fishing are an investment that can save you hours of frustration later on.

The approach.

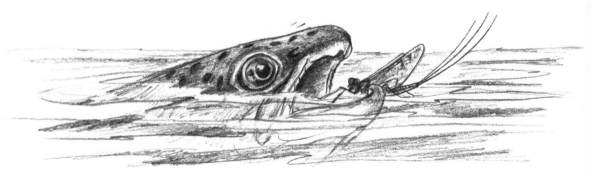

The first thing you should look for, of course, is rising fish. If a reasonable amount of surface feeding is going on, there is only one more step to take before you commence casting. All you now need to learn either by observation or by the capture of samples is what the fish are feeding on.

The examination of captured insects, their identification, and the selection of the proper imitation are the subjects of the following chapter, but the observation of trout rise forms and what they can tell you is too important to be passed over lightly. Many times fish will be taking insect forms an inch or so underwater, and it's easy to be misled into thinking that they're surface feeding. Only close scrutiny of the situation can keep you from misreading the resultant surface boils, but even if you make this mistake, all is not lost. Fish feeding this close to the skin of the water will usually take a floating imitation well anyway.

True surface takes in fast or choppy water are the hardest to read. Most of the time what you see is the splash made by the slap of the fish's tail as it dives for the bottom, and it is difficult to make subtle distinctions under these conditions.

Medium- and slow-water rises are easier to interpret. A small sip with a residual bubble should tell you that the fish are feeding on insects that are trapped and helpless in the surface film. These may be ants, jassids, spent or dead mayflies, or any number of terrestrial insects. Only examination of the water itself will tell you the exact type, size, and species.

When hatching mayfly duns are being eaten, the rise form is usually more obvious; the fish have to reach up a bit to take these insect forms. As a result, they show part of their head or head and shoulders and leave a more pronounced surface disturbance.

Medium-slow rise; residual bubble.

Trout catching caddis; splashy violent rise form.

The splashiest and most violent rise forms are almost always made when trout are feeding on hatching or egg-laying caddis. Most caddis species shoot up to the suface to hatch, and because egg-layers are hyperactive the trout have to slash quickly to take them. A word of caution though. Trout will sometimes take a departing mayfly dun in the same manner, so don't diagnose caddis as the meal-of-the-day unless slashing rises are the general pattern.

At any rate, as long as fish are rising often and regularly, the dry-fly man is in his element, and we'll leave you in this ideal situation for a while and turn our attention to more common, though less fortunate, conditions.

Most of the time, unhappily, you will be faced with the bleaker prospect of no fish or only a few small ones rising. Unless you've fished that particular piece of water at that time of day and period of year so frequently that you know all its secrets, you'll have to start thinking like a fish to catch a fish on the dry fly.

The first thought that should now enter your mind is whether you should fish on top or try some other fly-fishing method. Let's face it—as much as most anglers prefer to see a fish rise to the surface, there are times when chances of taking a fish on the dry are virtually impossible. If, in the face of no visible evidence of surface feeding, you decide to stick to the floating fly anyway, you'll be wise to spend even more time in observation and calculation before you wade into unfamiliar waters and start flailing away.

The single most important question to be answered—and the most difficult—is: Where will the good fish be lying? This is pivotal to your possible success, because dry-fly fishing is not only the most deliberate

Trout feeding in choppy-fast water.

and enjoyable form of fly fishing, but it is also the method that covers the *least* amount of water. If you're prospecting the water blindly, this sharply reduces your chances of placing the fly where a good fish will see it.

When fishing stillwater lakes and ponds you've never seen before, you're up against one of the toughest situations. Will the fish, whether bass, trout, or whatever, be in shallow bays, off middepth rocky points, or sulking in the depths? I wouldn't begin to give you advice here unless I knew the body of water intimately. Suffice it to say that if it's fairly early or late in the year and either early or late in the day, there should be some fish in reasonably shallow water where most of the feed is; whether you decide to prospect, follow a hunch, or discipline yourself to wait for a fish to reveal itself, you should have a chance of taking some fish on the dry. Local advice, if you can get it, or personal experience, if you happen to have it, are the most valuable aids under these conditions.

Trout feeding on hatching duns.

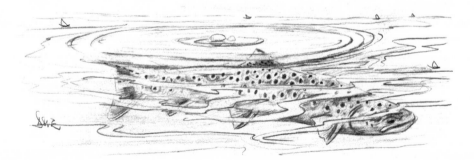

Fortunately, running water doesn't hide its secrets as well from the visiting angler. Since most streams and rivers are comparatively shallow, you can often tell the depth of various sections by actual observation of the bottom. Add to this the clues you can pick up by watching the disturbances the flow leaves on the water surface, and you should be able to put together enough evidence to locate a few fish even if none are willing to give themselves up by showing on the surface. If you're going to be fishing a particular stretch for a day or more, you have one more stratagem. You can walk through that portion of the stream at midday, when the light is best and the fishing worst, and pick out at close range the most likely lies—and sometimes even the fish themselves.

The species of fish you are out to catch also dictates, to a certain extent, where you should fish. Atlantic salmon are the most difficult fish for an angler to find without expert or local help. As a general rule, salmon will lie in what trouters would call a deep run rather than in a classic pool, but this is not a hard and fast rule. However, since it's virtually impossible to fish for Atlantics on this side of the ocean without a guide, due to Canadian law, pinpointing the lies of salmon is not a prime concern of this chapter.

Bass—and this usually means smallmouths in running water—are reasonably predictable, although they can surprise you from time to time. You can expect them to lie in water slightly slower than ideal trout water, both in slacker parts of pools and in calm pockets of the rapids. The largest bass will almost always live in the deepest pools, but these are also the bass you are least likely to rise to a dry fly unless you are fishing after dark.

Trout don't abide by the rules either, and to further complicate matters there are three main species of trout with three different lifestyles to consider. Again, each species does not always obey the rules

Making showy head-and-shoulder rise.

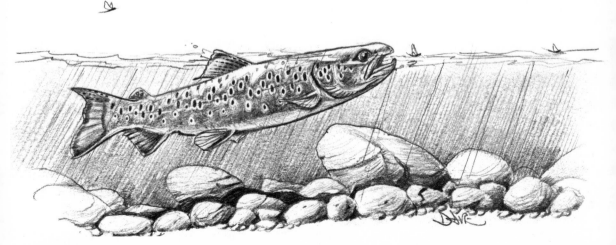

Rainbow in typical water.

laid down for it, but knowledge of the general characteristics can be helpful to the angler.

Rainbow trout will choose faster flowing water than the other two species. Rapid, narrow runs provide choice lies for this trout, and you'll even raise them in choppy white water where you can barely float your fly.

Brown trout prefer slightly slower currents. If I could fish only one type of water for browns, I would certainly pick all the places near the heads of pools where the water starts to lose its chop and fan out into the widening belly of the pool.

Brook trout will select lies where the flow is a bit more stately. This is especially true of the better class of fish. Tiddlers may station themselves in rapids and surprisingly thin water, but older fish prefer a more leisurely pace of flow.

Brown holding in typical water.

Brook trout in typical water.

Don't take this to mean that you won't occasionally find a splendid brookie in the chute at the head of a pool or that you won't rise a bragging rainbow in dead-slow water. The rules are general and based on percentages, but you shouldn't follow them slavishly.

Factors other than species are involved here too. In the early season, when the water is cold and fish are just leaving their wintering quarters, most of them will be in the deeper, slower stretches. A similar, but less pronounced, situation is likely to occur in fall too. On the other hand, during the heat of summer all fish—salmon, bass, and trout—may tend to crowd up into the rapids where there's more oxygen, despite their usual preferences.

Time of day affects trout position. Comfort and oxygen availability may exert their influences; so does availability of food. Rapids may be happy hunting grounds at midday, but profuse falls of spent flies or dying egg-layers may draw fish to the easy feeding at the slow tail ends of pools at dusk.

This latter factor of availability of food may be the most important to dry-fly fishermen. Fish may hide or hold in any number of secure places, but when they feed they must station themselves where the food is. When you are considering prime prospects—trout of three to six years of age, or usually those of from 10 to 18 inches—your best chance of taking them is when hunger or food supply has urged them to take up feeding stations where insects of some kind are readily accessible.

This is where the observant and experienced dry-fly man can cash in. Certain portions of a river, at predictable times of day and year, will bunch insect-interested fish in areas where the dry-fly man can exploit his art. Even if the fish are not rising enthusiastically at these times, a knowledgeable fly fisherman can take his toll at some time or place during almost any fishing day.

Determining where the food and the fish will be from visual clues left by the current is known as the art of "reading the water," and it is one of the dry-fly man's most important skills. The ideal lie for river fish is one that offers food, comfort, and safety, and when you find a stretch or even a small pocket that offers all three, it is wise to work it over thoroughly before moving on.

The path of food—insects drifting in or on top of the current—in flowing water is quite predictable. Where the current from, say, a ten-foot-wide section of flow is funneled into a run only a foot or so wide, it's obvious that a lot of food will be coming through that narrow slot. If such a place is not too far from a safe retreat, you can expect a good fish—or several—to be stationed there. It is this simple principle of concentration of food in the flow that explains why deep, narrow runs and the outside portions of river bends are almost always highly productive to the fly fisher.

Comfort is a factor that affects fish position all year long. In winter and during very cold spells in spring and fall, fish will seek deep, slow water, as we have said, to conserve energy. On the other hand, when river water gets a bit too warm for their comfort, fish will seek out spots where cool springs or small brooks enter the river or will edge up into the fast white water where there is also more oxygen. Sheets of shallow, smooth water, where a fish would have to swim rapidly to hold his own against the current, are seldom tenanted, because a fish would expend more energy here than he could hope to replace from the available food supply.

Safety is seldom far from a trout's thoughts—or perhaps I should say instincts. Except when they're feeding most gluttonously, fish will seldom stray far from a safe retreat. This may be an overhanging bush, an undercut bank, an irregular rock ledge, a small space under a flat rock, or merely water so relatively deep that it offers security from predators above.

River fish live a life of constant peril, and they have their escape routes and hideouts carefully memorized. One of the best ways to prove this to yourself (and, by the way, to learn more about trout habits) is to walk slowly down the center of a small stream and watch the fish dart away at your approach. This will not only reveal where the fish tend to feed in that stretch—useful knowledge for the next time you fish there—but it should convince you that the most popular feeding stations lie close to sanctuaries.

Now, after all this general discussion of fish habits and preferences, let's get back to the visiting angler, who is rigged up and waiting to start fishing. Even though few or no fish are rising, the above information should enable him to choose productive water for his dry-fly prospecting. He now knows *where* to make his entry. But perhaps he could use a little advice on *how* to do it.

Slow-flowing portions of streams and still waters offer the wading angler the toughest challenge. The actual act of wading is easiest and safest under these conditions; this is often the chief trouble. One tends to waltz in and head for the chosen casting position like a bull moose in mating season. Don't do it! The ripples you send out will probably alert or even scatter every fish within possible casting distance that's thinking about feeding. Ease in gently and glide as slowly as possible to your casting position, and once there, try your hardest to cast without moving your body or sluffing your legs; either of these two common acts will send out warning ripples.

How close should you approach the suspected lie of a fish in slow water? In part this will be dictated by the clarity of that particular body of water. Cloudy or stained water will obviously allow a fairly close approach. If the water is clear, however, you'll have to reach out longer. This doesn't mean you should put on a tournament casting exhibition, but do show the fish respect instead of your threatening head and torso. A good rule of thumb is to estimate how far away you could see a fish (and it, you) and then add 10 feet to your casting distance.

Faster water may cover up most of the clumsiness in your wading as far as the fish are concerned, but you, the angler, are more likely to take a dunking. *Do* wear felt, hobs, or chains on the bottoms of your boots or waders under these conditions. And even then it's wise to follow a few general rules that can help you avoid an uncomfortable, and perhaps dangerous, fall.

Be sure one foot is securely anchored on stable bottom before you move the other one. Where the water is swift, walk sideways to it, with one leg almost directly upstream of the other. You offer less current resistance in this position. And don't, repeat don't, try to tiptoe across the tops of submerged rocks or boulders when you're navigating in deep water. Such footholds are sure to be slippery, and when you're up to your boot- or wader-tops, you've already given away any margin for error.

Despite the tougher wading conditions, fast water offers the fly fisherman certain advantages over the fish. The crinkled surface allows a close approach to the selected lies which makes for accurate casting and

The approach; Len Wright.

dragfree floats; even hooking the fish is easier. How close is close? In fast runs or broken pocket water, twenty to twenty-five feet is often far enough away from a fish if you are fishing upcurrent. No matter how much you love to lay out a long line with your favorite rod, you'll catch far more fish in fast or broken water if you work with a short line.

So there you are, standing safely, quietly, and undetected within optimum casting range of either a free-rising front or a fishy-looking lie. The size and pattern of fly you tie on, how you cast it, and the manner in which you present it will have to wait for the expert advice in subsequent chapters.

Meanwhile, I'd love to be in your boots. You couldn't be in a more enviable position.

| *My Favorite Places to Fish* | *Type of Fish* | *Best Time* | *Suggested Flies* | |
			Type	*Size*
Beaverkill, Roscoe, New York, to East Branch, New York	Brown	May 1–June 1	1. Red Quill 2. Fluttering Caddis (dun) 3. Gray Fox Variant	14, 16 14 12, 14
East Branch of Delaware River, Hankins, New York, upstream for several miles	Brown Rainbow	April 20– June 1	1. Dun Variant 2. Adams 3. Gray Fox Variant	12 14, 16 12
Housatonic River, Cornwall Bridge, Connecticut	Brown	April 15– June 1	1. Red Quill 2. March Brown 3. Dun Variant	14, 16 12 12
Miramichi River, twenty miles either side of Doaktown, New Brunswick, Canada	Atlantic salmon	July and early August	1. White Wulff 2. Bomber 3. Irresistible	8 8 L.S. 8
Eagle River, Labrador	Atlantic salmon	Late July and early August	1. White Wulff 2. Bomber 3. Irresistible	8 8 L.S. 8

Carl E. Richards moved from Ohio to Michigan to practice dentistry and trout-fish. Today he is considered by many authorities to be one of the outstanding fly fishermen in the United States.

When he was teamed with Doug Swisher, their careful observations of mayflies and other aquatic insects led to their development of the Swisher-Richards patterns, now known across the country. As an adviser to the American League of Anglers, he contributes to conservation.

His writings have appeared in numerous periodicals, and he is a co-author of Selective Trout *and* Fly Fishing Strategy. *He also is a contributing author in* Art Flick's Master Fly Tying Guide.

8. Hatches and Imitations
Mayflies, Caddis, Midges, and Stone Flies

Carl E. Richards

WHY STUDY ENTOMOLOGY? Must we become Latin scholars in order to become accomplished dry-fly fishers? Is it really that important?

The answer to the latter is an emphatic yes, it is very important! The study of entomology will help us catch more fish and more good fish than otherwise would be possible. Just a basic knowledge of the hatching and egg-laying activities of trout stream insects will allow us to select the artificial that closely resembles the naturals on which fish are feeding at any given time and to fish that artificial in an enticing, realistic manner. How deeply one delves into the discipline is, of course, a personal choice. Some will become engrossed in the study for its own sake, since entomology can be almost as interesting as fly fishing itself. Others will desire only the basics, which will at least allow them to choose the right fly at the right time and to become more successful fish-catchers. A certain minimum knowledge, however, is essential to fish the hatches successfully and that, I feel, is what dry-fly fishing is really all about—fishing the hatch. The study need not be too involved, but certain elementary facts must be learned and committed to memory or one will be helpless when trout are feeding selectively.

In my travels around the country I find that many anglers, and even some veterans, know little about basic trout stream insects. This limits their fish-taking ability drastically. To me, the study of aquatic entomology is at least half the fun of fly fishing. I admit it is not necessary for an angler to be able to differentiate between a male *Siphlonurus occidentalis* subimago and a female *Siphlonurus quebecinsis* imago to be successful, but he should at least know the difference between a mayfly and a stone fly. He should also know the difference between a mayfly dun and a mayfly spinner, be able to recognize what is on the water at a given time, and select an appropriate imitation that will fool some fish. So, though you don't need to become a Latin scholar, you do need to become a practical entomologist.

Let me illustrate how helpful a little familiarity with the hatches can be. About a month ago I was fishing Michigan's incredibly rich Au Sable on a warm June evening. It was about an hour before dusk, a small caddis hatch was in progress, and the fish were taking a size 18 Henryville Special with splashy enthusiasm. I noticed a young fellow downstream who appeared to be casting fairly well but was not hooking any fish. As I waded closer to his position, he asked what the fish were taking and I told him. He was obviously a beginner and had no notion of the correct fly to use to imitate a caddis hatch, so I presented him with a Henryville Special. I explained that a little later on the hatch would switch to a small, yellow stone fly, and then, just at dark, a size 16 Pale Evening dun would appear. I picked out two suitable patterns from his fly box and proceeded on my way. After dark, as I waded back to the car, I encountered the young angler, who made up in enthusiasm what he lacked in experience. He was astounded that I was able to predict which insects would hatch and what patterns would take fish at such a precise time. He had been camped in the area for three days and until then had been unable to hook even one fish. He had been casting over hundreds of risers for three evenings without taking any of them.

It was easy for me because I had been there before. However, if he had only known the difference between an adult caddis, an adult stone fly, and a mayfly spinner, he could have easily captured a specimen, matched the size and color with the correct type fly, and he would have been catching fish from the first day. That is what I am going to explain in this chapter: how to recognize the basic orders of aquatic insects, how to capture one when fish are feeding during a hatch, and how to pick an imitation that is the correct size, color, and shape.

Certain basic types of aquatic insects make up the major portion of the trout's diet. The four main insect orders that emerge from our trout streams and lakes in degree of their importance are: mayflies (Ephemeroptera), caddis flies (Trichoptera), midges (Diptera), and stone flies (Plecoptera).

All four orders belong to the class Insecta. The practical entomologist should understand basic biological classification. All living things are classified plant or animal. All members of the plant or animal kingdom are classified under categories that progress from the general to the specific. An example would be the famous Brown Drake, found in both the East and the West:

Kingdom: Animal
Subkingdom: Invertebrate (all animals without backbones)
Phylum: Arthropoda (all animals with bilateral symmetry, external
                skeletons, and jointed legs)
Class: Insecta (all true insects)
Order: Ephemeroptera (all mayflies)
Family: Ephemeridae (all true burrowing mayflies)
Genus: Ephemera (a group of related burrowing mayflies)
Species: Simulans (a particular kind of burrowing mayfly, which
                can interbreed)

To be an effective hatchmaker you must at least be able to differentiate between adult mayflies, caddis flies, midges, stone flies, and all the immature stages of each of these orders, and do so rather quickly. Many hatches and most spinner falls do not last very long. You do not have time to try four or five patterns on a trial-by-error basis. Rather, you should be able to choose the right fly at the right time; only then can you be suitably equipped to hook your share of fish on the dry fly.

MAYFLY

The mayfly (*Ephemeroptera*) is the single most important order of trout stream insect. All mayflies have two large, upright wings, two or three tails, and most have two very small hind wings. They look like little sailboats floating in the current and are the only trout stream insects with upright wings. The life cycle is: egg, nymph, dun (subimago), spinner (imago).

(left) *Mayfly nymphs:* A. *Burrowing.* B. *Swimming.* (right) *Mayfly dun.*

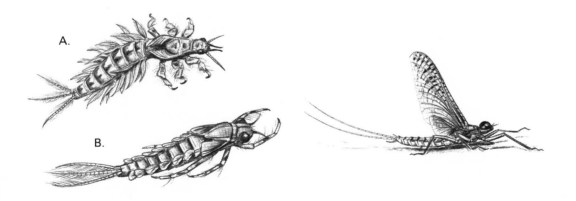

A.

B.

CHRISTINE FONG

Mayfly nymph changing to dun.

The Nymph. The eggs hatch into an underwater form called a nymph, which usually lasts about a year but may last two months to two years or more, depending on the species. They range in size from 3 to 36 mm. or more and have three tails (rarely two) and gills emitting from the side of the middle segments of the abdomen. The nymphs grow from a very small size through progressively larger stages, each stage accompanied by a molt and each called an instar. They vary greatly in shape, depending on the ecosystem they have become adapted to, such as fast or slow water. Most are dirty tan to brown in color with a lighter underside, but they can vary from cream to olive to black.

The Emergence. When the nymph is fully grown it swims to the surface and changes into a winged fly called a dun (subimago) by splitting its nymphal skin and emerging from it. The dun rests on the surface, drying its wings, and then flies away to nearby trees or meadows. This entire procedure is called the hatch. At this time the nymphs and the duns are extremely vulnerable. Before and during the hatch a standard fur-bodied type of mayfly nymph of the correct size and color is a good imitation. During the hatch a mayfly dun imitation such as a Sidewinder No Hackle dun is my personal choice.

A standard hackle pattern can be fairly effective if tied sparsely, that is, with the hackle very short (one half the length of the body) and two or three turns only, although it presents an inferior outline. The fur body is what really floats the fly in both the No Hackle dun and the sparse standard pattern. I always use 3X fine-wire hooks, which are a great help in flotation.

One of the most deadly patterns of all during an emergence is the floating nymph. A few years ago I purchased a stomach pump made especially for this purpose and learned, to my great surprise, how ignorant I was about how trout feed during a rise. During first sessions with the pump, I selected a good fish which was feeding regularly on the surface and which I believed to be taking only duns. On examining the stomach contents I found these trout invariably took two or three nymphs for each floating dun. It was not nymphs at the beginning of the hatch and duns toward the end, as we had all been taught. It is my belief trout prefer the floating nymphs because they have more time to capture the nymph. The dun, after all, can fly away at any time but the nymph cannot.

The Spinner Fall. After the dun has dried its wings and flown to the trees, it rests for a period of a few hours to a few days and then undergoes a final molt into a spinner or imago. *Ephemeroptera* is the only one of the four important orders that undergoes a molt after attaining the winged stage. The dun is a drab insect with dull, opaque wings and tails, approximately equal in length to the body. The spinner is, by contrast, bright and shiny, with long tails (twice as long as the body) and clear transparent wings. The spinners return to the river, mate in a swarm usually over riffles, and fall spent into the stream after egg-

Mayfly spinner.

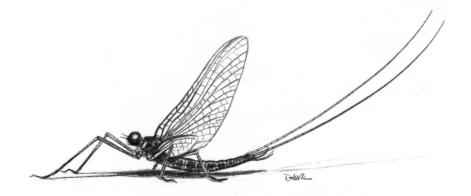

(above and below) *Metamorphosis of mayfly dun to spinner.*

laying. At this time (the spinner fall), the correct imitation is a half-spent or full-spent mayfly spinner imitation. My personal choice is a hen spinner in the correct size and shape.

Spinner falls occur more often in the evening or at dark but can happen during the morning hours, depending again upon the species and, of course, the weather. There are approximately one hundred twenty *Ephemeroptera* species of major importance to the fly fisherman in the United States, and with a little observation you will quickly become familiar with the important ones in your area. Usually one

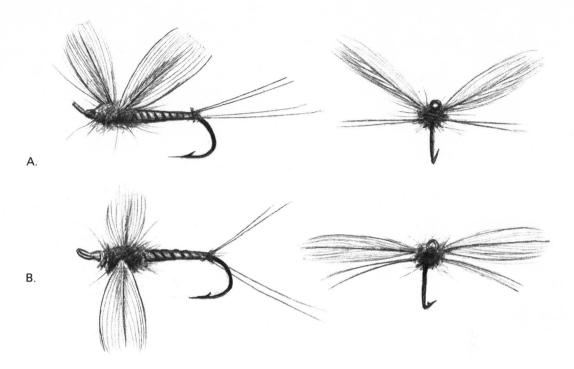

Patterns of hen spinners: A. *Half spent.* B. *Full spent.*

stream or geographic area has only about ten to fifteen species that are of great interest to the average fly fisher.

As a general rule, early in the season (March–May) mayflies tend to be dark in color: dark gray wings and dark brown or olive bodies. Later, as the lighter yellows and greens appear, the insects become lighter in color, most likely to blend in with the background and escape their many predators. The wings become pale gray and the bodies yellow and pale buff or olive. Then in September and October the flies become darker again. As the autumn leaves turn dark, so do the insects.

CADDIS FLIES (TRICHOPTERA)

Caddis flies are also very important trout stream insects, and in some locations they are even more numerous than mayflies. They can easily be distinguished by their four wings of nearly equal length which are covered with tiny hairs and, when at rest, are carried in an inverted V or tent over the back. They are usually medium to small in size (14–24) and have no tails. There are over one thousand known species on this continent.

The life cycle of a caddis differs from the mayfly and follows this order: egg, larva, pupa, adult. The eggs are deposited in or near the water, eventually hatching into a worm which may or may not build a case, depending on the species. Two large groups of caddis larvae exist. One group builds a case or house (evidently for protection and camouflage) in which the larva lives. These cases can be constructed of practically any material such as twigs, stones, and bits of leaf or bark. The other caddis are free-living, meaning they range about the bottom of the stream without cases. When matured the larva makes a cocoon (much like a caterpillar) in which it changes into a pupa. When the pupa is fully developed, it cuts its way out of the cocoon and migrates to the surface. Some species crawl out of the water to emerge, and some drift in the film until the pupal skin is broken and the adult flies away. The adult caddis are able to live much longer than mayflies, as they can absorb water. Most species mate at rest, so the females are the ones taken at egg-laying time. The eggs are deposited on the water, on vegetation overhanging the water, or underwater by diving females.

During a caddis hatch three imitations are effective. Due to the drifting of the pupa in the film before emergence, a pupal imitation is often deadly. The stillborn adult, which is a pattern tied to imitate a fly stuck halfway out of the shuck, is, in my experience, the most deadly of all the patterns during an emergence. The Henryville Special is good at hatch time and during the egg-laying flight. A spent caddis is effective at the end of the fall.

(left) *Caddis flies:* A. *Larva.* B. *Pupa.* C. *Stillborn.* (right) *Caddis fly imitations:* A. *Latex worm.* B. *Latex pupa.* C. *Stillborn.* D. *Henryville.*

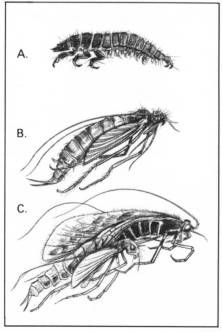
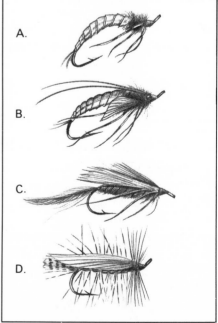

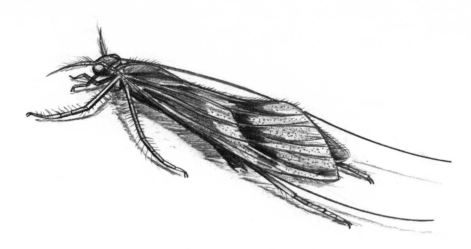

Adult caddis fly.

Of course, the angler must match the size and color of the artificial with the natural. As with all flies, this cannot be done by observing the natural on the wing; a specimen must be captured and examined in the hand. Adult caddis flies are jumpy and wary, thus rather difficult to capture. Often a net is required. Caddis flies are attracted to bright lights, however, and during the evening your car lights can be a good collecting spot. With so many species existing, most anglers do not bother to identify this order precisely as to species. It is enough to be aware of the five main colors—tan, gray, olive, cream, dark brown—and to have reasonable imitations in sizes from 14–20.

MIDGES (DIPTERA)

These flies have only two short wings (shorter than the body), which lie flat along the top of the body usually slightly to the side in a V, and possess no tails. Most are small, sizes 22–28, and even smaller. The life cycle goes egg, larva, pupa, adult. At hatch time the pupa ascends to the surface where it drifts for a time; the winged insect then emerges and flies away.

During the hatch a pupa or stillborn artificial are usually effective; a hackled adult type can be used later during the emergence or at the egg-laying flight.

These flies are especially important to trout in slower-moving water such as spring creeks and limestone streams. Some lake species are fairly large. They are rarely of much importance in faster currents. This is a very large and diverse group; they can be almost any color, but black and olive are common. When trout are feeding on midges, they

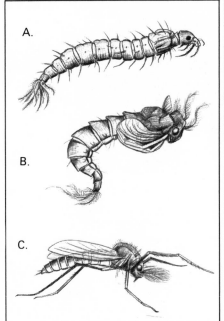
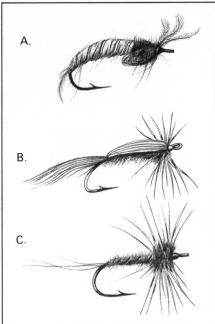

(left) *Midges:* A. *Larva.* B. *Pupa.* C. *Adult.* (right) *Midge imitations:* A. *Pupa fly.* B. *Stillborn fly.* C. *Hackled adult.*

can be extremely selective. Exact size in the artificial is often critical. An error of a single size (20 instead of 22) can mean a discrepancy of over 30 percent, and almost always this is too great for the critical eye of a brown trout. To be effective, close imitations are necessary!

STONE FLIES (PLECOPTERA)

This rather small order of flies is of very little importance in slow waters, yet in turbulent, rocky streams, such as the Madison and the Big Hole, they provide the largest flies and the most spectacular fishing of the season. In certain streams in Oregon they are the second most important trout food. Stone flies vary in size from very large to very small (2–20). Adults have four long wings, which are hard, shiny, heavily veined, and held flat over the back when at rest.

The life cycle goes egg, nymph, adult. The generally flatish nymphs are readily distinguished from mayfly nymphs since they have only two short tails with rather long antennae, no gills on the abdomen, and two equal wing cases. When the nymph is mature, most species (but by no means all) crawl to land and emerge. They mate at rest and return a few days to a few weeks later to lay their eggs.

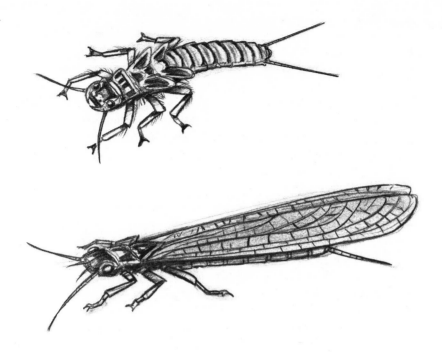

Stone flies: (top) *Nymph.* (bottom) *Adult.*

The emergence is important only in those species that emerge in water, and they are best imitated by a combination latex and fur stone fly nymph or a down-hairwing dry imitation. The egg-layers are well imitated by an adult stone fly artificial with a lot of hackle to stimulate moving wings. Many of the medium and small stones are yellow with a few showing olive, tan, and dark brown. Usually the underside of the nymph is much lighter than the top.

Imitation adult stone fly.

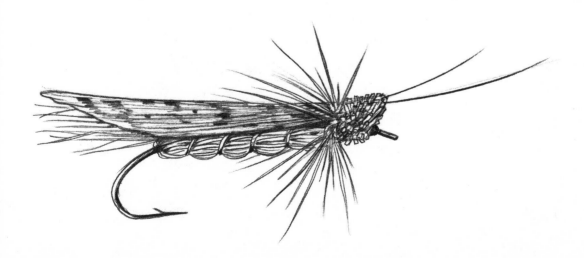

Trout, of course, feed on many other food items besides the four major orders listed above. Although these other orders are normally of lesser importance, when they are numerous fish will feed on them selectively, so a few representative imitations should be carried for shrimp, beetles, spiders, moths, crane flies, grasshoppers, ants, dragon flies, damselflies, and scuds. Some of the above are not aquatic but terrestrial, and some are not even insects but crustaceans.

SELECTING AN ARTIFICIAL

Now that we have the preceding pages firmly in mind, we can distinguish between all the stages of all the naturals, and know what pattern types to tie on to imitate the various stages of the four major orders of aquatic insects. How do we translate this knowledge into a fishing situation? Imagine you are in the middle of a pool with fish rising all around, flies buzzing in the air and drifting on the currents. How do you select the correct imitation? That's the meat of this chapter—how to pick an artificial at the right time which will take fish when trout are rising to naturals. It can be easy if you are not rattled by the feeding fish. The first thing to do is find out what type or order of insect is on the water, and this is done by capturing one and examining it closely in the hand, preferably with an 8X or a 10X glass. If the flies are on the water, a simple tropical fish aquarium net can be dipped onto the flow, and the

Natural fly being trapped in hand net.

current will carry the specimen into the net. If the fly is in the air, a simple net such as that sold by the Orvis Company in their entomology kit can be fixed to the tip of the fly rod and used as a butterfly net.

Once the specimen is in the hand, the order and stage is determined (e.g., mayfly nymph, dun, or spinner). Then an artificial of the correct size, shape, coloration, and type is selected from the fly box, and you should be in business quickly and logically. This whole process takes place in the heat of battle, however, and a certain calm deduction is required. Most people get so excited by splashing trout that they take a wild guess as to the correct pattern and immediately begin to flail the water. They normally end up exhausted, frustrated, and fishless. To be successful you must remain calm, patiently obtain a specimen, and know a mayfly has upright wings, a caddis has tent-shaped wings, a stone has flat wings over the body, and a midge has flat, V-shaped wings (flat but to the side of the body), and you must know which artificial type works when each natural is on the water. If you are thoroughly familiar with these facts, you will be light years ahead of the majority of dry-fly anglers and much more effective!

THE MULTIPLE HATCH

I have just described a simple hatch where only one or at the most two insects are hatching at a time. Any observant fly fisher with a little knowledge of practical entomology should be able to choose his pattern and do well at the rise or the spinner fall. A much more difficult experience will be had during a multiple hatch. At times, especially on rich streams, many different types of insects can be on the water at the same time. On the lime-rich Rogue near my home, I have seen midges, caddis, stones, crane flies, and four mayfly species, both duns and spinners simultaneously. During a multiple hatch such as this, trout usually feed selectively on one of the types.

How do we select the right fly? This is a difficult problem even for the veteran anglers; the answer is never simple. Experience, knowledge, and close observation is required. A few bits of information should be of help. First, trout will usually feed on the insect present in the greatest numbers. Quite often a small fly will be present in company with a large fly but in much greater number; the fish will feed on the smaller fly exclusively, though the inexperienced angler usually tries the larger fly first. Try to decide which natural is most numerous. If a suitable imitation does not work within five minutes, look again and try another idea. Do not keep casting uselessly with the same pattern.

Next, try to identify the rise form and relate that to a fly type. Trout will rise very quietly and deliberately to insect forms which are smaller and cannot escape, such as medium to small mayfly spinners. The larger and more escape-prone the insect, the more hurried and splashy the rise. Therefore, if you observe that size 12 Green Drake duns and size 18 Baetis spinners are both on the water and the rise forms are quiet dimples, the obvious choice would be size 18 Hen Spinner in the correct color. Conversely, a violent rise form would indicate a size 12 Sidewinder dun to imitate the Green Drake.

These multiple hatches can be mystifying, so don't be discouraged by a few failures. One of the most pleasing aspects of dry-fly fishing is its complexity. I, for one, would soon tire of constant success, and multiple hatches certainly ensure against that. However, the practical entomologist will have a fighting chance at a solution to the problem; the uninformed will be all but helpless. A thorough study of practical aquatic entomology will pay huge dividends at hatch time.

My Favorite Places to Fish	*Type of Fish*	*Best Time*	*Suggested Flies*	
			Type	*Size*
Au Sable River, Michigan	Brown Brook Rainbow	May June July	1. Slate Tan No Hackle 2. Slate Olive No Hackle 3. White/Black Hen Spinner	14 18 26
Henrys Fork, Snake River, Idaho	Rainbow	June– September	1. Green Drake 2. Speckled Spinner 3. White/Black Hen Spinner	12 16 22
Armstrong Spring Creek, Montana	Brown	July August September	1. Gray/Yellow No Hackle 2. Black Midge 3. Olive Midge	16, 18 22 24
Pere Marquette River, Michigan	Steelhead	October March April	1. Single Egg Fly 2. Royal Coachman streamer	6 4
Ungava Peninsula, Quebec, Canada	Atlantic salmon	August– September	1. Yellow stone fly (dry) 2. Black stone fly (dry) 3. Bomber (dry)	4 4 4

Charlie Fox has been carrying on a love affair with trout since early boyhood. Born in Harrisburg, Pennsylvania, he spent many days of his youth along Yellow Breeches Creek near the Susquehanna River. In later years he moved near the Letort and, with Vince Marinaro, became one of the originators of angling with terrestrial imitations and analyzing the feeding habits of trout.

As a fisherman, he now divides his time between salmon, trout, bass, and muskies.

His work for conservation has been outstanding. He represented his state on Project 70 (the woods and waters of hundreds of thousands of Pennsylvania's acres) and has been an inspiration as adviser to the American League of Anglers and Trout Unlimited.

In the literary world he served as editor of the Pennsylvania Angler *and the outdoor division of Stackpole Books. Besides appearing in numerous periodicals, he is the author of* This Wonderful World of Trout *and* Rising Trout.

9. Upstream, the Classic Presentation

History, the Cast, Drag, and Curves

Charles K. Fox

LET A DRY FLY be substituted for the wet one, the line switched a few times through the air to throw off its superabundant moisture, a judicious cast made just above the rising fish, and the flow allowed to float it towards and over them, and the chances are ten to one that it is seized as readily as the living insect. This dry fly, we must remark, should be an imitation of the natural fly on which the fish is feeding.

These words were published in 1851 by G.P.R. Pulman in his *Vade Mecum of Fly Fishing for Trout,* and to this day nobody has written a better description of classic dry-fly presentation.

But another man popularized this upstream cast and for years, especially in England, made it sacrosanct. He was George Selwyn Marryat, about whom Lord Grey of Fallodon, my angling idol and favorite author, wrote in his classic *Fly Fishing:*

Sometimes, too, but not often, we saw at "Old Barge" the greatest angler I have ever met. One could not say which was more instructive, to watch his fishing or to listen to his talk; no one had more information to give, no one was more generous in giving it; his knowledge seemed the result of not only observation and experience, but of some peculiar insight into the ways of trout. In the management of rod and tackle he displayed not only skill but genius.

Master angler Marryat would not write a book; instead he chose as his prophet and historian a scholar-angler and flytier, Frederic M. Halford.

The classic upstream dry-fly cast.

Halford's *Floating Flies and How to Dress Them* was published in 1880; a more famous work, *Dry Fly Fishing in Theory and Practice*, was published three years later.

Floating Flies emphasized the fecundity of emerging fly life on British streams and stressed the importance of good imitations floated *down*stream on the gentle currents. *Dry Fly Fishing* established the straight upstream cast as the only possible and only permitted method to fish for trout. Bonded by this heritage, even today upstream casts are still the "only thing" in England, where regular chalk stream practice was and is to watch for, locate, and then fish exclusively to the rise of a brown trout.

In America most streams are fast-flowing and stony. In earlier years they were inhabited by native brook trout, the most beautiful trout that swims, as opposed to brown trout, the smartest fish that swims, which inhabited the placid, weeded streams in England. In 1884 brown trout were introduced to this country, and today, except for the smaller brooks, they have taken over most of our waters. Fortunately, this change of environment did not alter their marvelous habit of rising to take food from the surface film. The difference was that emerging insect life in our waters was never as prevalent as fly life in England, so our fishermen had to develop new techniques. If there were no rises, casts were made to likely spots, hoping that a hungry trout would be waiting and watching. If the current was slow near the shore and faster in the middle, curve casts had to be thrown. If fish did not rise on the first pass, a hatch was "created" by repeated casts.

The classic dry-fly approach in both fishing the water and fishing the rise was the foundation for all these variations. The dictum still is: *Deliver the fly so that it drifts naturally over the adjudged hot spot, just as an insect would ride the water.*

This means that the dry-fly fisherman faces upstream, casts upstream, and lets the current carry the fly back to him naturally, at the same time keeping the line away from the fish. If you are a neophyte and if you are right-handed, you should fish from the left side looking upstream.

Every dry-fly angler is faced with two challenges—accuracy and natural float. Inaccuracy is a time-waster; unnatural float, which generations of anglers have regarded as an abomination and have distastefully called "drag," will make some fish so suspicious that they cannot be caught without first being rested. Thus, dry-fly fishing is a battle of caster versus drag every bit as much as it is fisherman versus fish.

The angler must constantly make counterdrag moves to obtain surer and longer floats—the classic drift. Like the baseball pitcher, he can resort to curves; like the baseball switch-hitter, he can operate from above either shoulder; but unlike the ballplayer, he can mend his line on the water between himself and the fly. The fisherman can make the fly kick back, creating a serpentine path the leader follows; he can wiggle or shake off extra line from the rod, creating a curving appearance of bows in the floating line beyond the rod tip. Casting skill is essential if we hope to deceive sophisticated fish.

Of the various control casts that make for longer free drifts of the fly, the kickback, in my judgment, is the most practical and useful. In this case the leader falls in a snakelike path, thus permitting a longer free float while the leader is straightening out.

Back in the glory days of Pennsylvania's Big Spring, a native brook trout stream, I visited it two or three evenings a week during the course of the season in the good company of Vince Marinaro. The surface was, for the most part, flat but of uneven flow. The beautiful trout were lined up in such a manner that with a long float it was possible on a single drift to show a fly to more than one fish. There were times when a trout would move under a fly to look it over, only to have a greedy brookie charge in ahead and take it. Competition between trout was an aid to fishing, for the longer the dragfree drift, the better one's chances became. We used the kickback cast practically all the time.

To obtain this snaky leader, one casts more by feel than by formula. The trick is to shoot too little line as opposed to the normal amount for the effort expended, as the rod tip is stopped at a high position. A slight jolt on the high rod is felt when the cast is just right, and the leader will fall to the water with many curves in a narrow path.

The all-important pickup from the left side looking upstream is a version of the roll cast. At the conclusion of the drift of the fly, the rod tip is pushed forward, making the line, leader, and fly roll up in the air. Before the line has a chance to land on the water, a high backcast is made. Now the fly is airborne and can be dried sufficiently by a series of false casts to make it float. Again it is put down on the water above the expected position of the fish to drift naturally into the window and over the trout. This roll pickup is extremely useful.

To accomplish the same thing while casting up and across from the right side of the stream, the roll pickup is made from over the left shoulder. If so desired, the false casting can be transferred to the right side following the first forward cast.

A favorite trout feeding place in most pools is at the tail end, where the water shallows out before breaking into a riffle. If the angler can cast from either corner of the tail of the pool, there is a classy little trick that will make possible a dragless drift over the trout before the broken water actually catches the line and drags the fly. The cast is made so that the fly will alight in front of the trout. Directly after it lands on the

Kickback cast: 1. Forward cast; a. fly moves forward with excess speed. 2. Kickback; rod is stopped and pulled back; b. line, leader, and fly fall in a snaky shape on water.

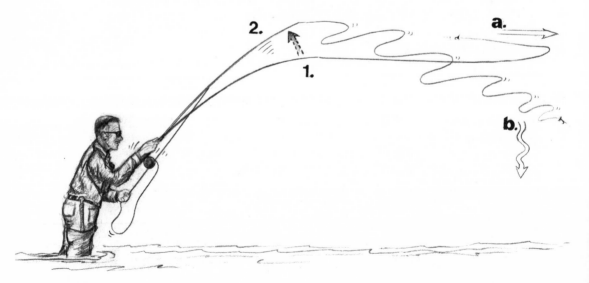

water, the angler rolls the close portion of his line out of the water and
with a rotary motion loops it upstream. From the left corner (as one
looks up), the roll is forehand; from the right corner, backhand. Sufficient force is used to roll the lower part of the line upstream and away
from the pull of the riffle, but not enough to move the fly. When advis-
able a second, and even a third, mend can be negotiated as the fly continues its natural drift.

The caster can manipulate his fly rod over either shoulder, which
means that such selectivity makes the avoidance of obstacles possible—
overhead foliage in particular—and he will still have room for false casting. There would be but little advantage in being ambidextrous. But
there is another reason for backhand casting.

Fast-fall, stony water features slicks and glides. There are times
when nature gives the angler the opportunity to fish the rise among the
rocks and other times when the fisherman simply searches the water
among the rocks for willing takers. In all rock-studded rivers there are
varying currents, and more frequently than not the fastest water is between the caster and his target. A curve cast in the appropriate direction
can bring about a longer drag-free drift. The most elementary way for a
right-hander to throw a curve to the right is to utilize a fly offering considerable air resistance, such as a variant or spider, and cast with the rod
tip lowered slightly. Air resistance will cause the line and leader to fall
into the shape of a shepherd's crook.

Roll cast pickup: 1. Conclusion of drift. 2. Rod pulled back to form loose loop.
3. Rod pushed forward in a power roll.

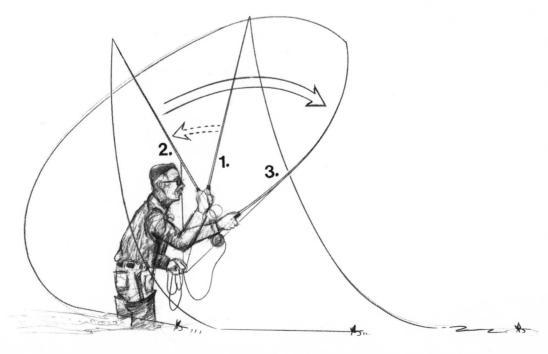

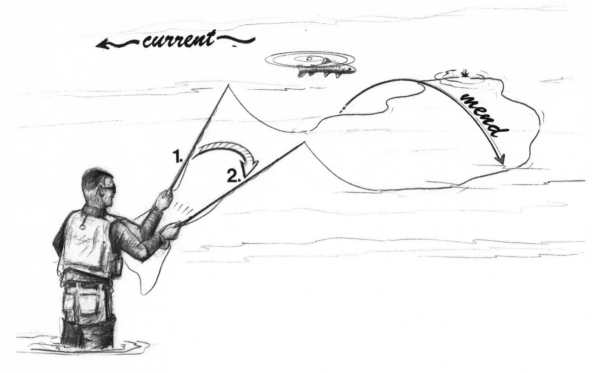

Mending line position on water: 1. Cast to spot above feeding trout. 2. With ro-tary motion upstream, line position is mended.

A cast over the other shoulder with the same fly will result in a loop to the left.

Another way for a right-hander to make a curve to the right, partic-ularly when a small fly is used, is to shoot slightly more line than the cast would normally justify.

The right-hander can execute a curve to the left by casting to the spot in the normal way, up to the point when the line begins to shoot, and then abruptly shoving the rod tip away from and parallel with the surface of the water. This causes the line and leader to curve away from the fly.

Sometimes a situation is such that reckless casting is required, and occasionally a bold cast pays off in abundant satisfaction. An instance of this was responsible for my learning how to cast a shepherd's crook to the left.

On my side of the stream was a small brushpile, creating an attrac-tive backwater in front of it. When one threw a live grasshopper into the water upstream, it was taken with confidence by a fine trout close to the brush. Because of the bushes it was not possible to present a fly to the brushpile fish from above, and the stream here could not be crossed in

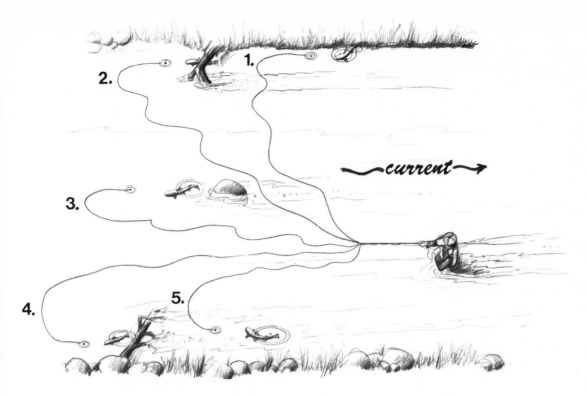

Curvecasting to right: 1. To fish feeding under bank. 2. To fish feeding under a log. 3. To fish feeding in front of a boulder. Curvecasting to left: 4. To fish feeding in front of a brush pile. 5. To fish feeding in slow eddy.

order to fish it from the other side. There remained one alternative: fish from below.

I had on at the time an Art Neumann imitation, which I depend upon in hopper time. With reckless abandon I cast in the air upstream over the brushpile. As the line and leader started to fall, I shoved the rod, tip, and butt toward midstream. I expected to tangle with the brushpile, but to my glee and surprise that was not the case. The midportion of the line dropped to the water beyond the end of the protruding snags as the upper part and the leader curved to the left in a manner that amazed me.

The fish was taken.

So, in the same manner, were some others on subsequent days.

But more to the point, I had learned how to pitch a good curve to the left, even when a large fly is used. The experience reminded me of the way I felt the day I discovered how to make a baseball curve.

In casting, force exerted on the butt of the rod creates distance—and also a wide loop on the backcast. The thrust and motion employed by the caster is comparable to hitting a nail with a hammer. Force administered to the rod tip diminishes the loop. Should the caster wish to drive his fly under overhanging foliage, he can tighten the loop by anchoring the casting elbow on his hip, casting with the *tip* of his rod, and shooting some line.

Many variations, all deriving from the upstream cast, are useful and at times necessary; in order to execute one or all of them, it is important to first master the basics.

Gradually accelerated motion is the key to good casting; without it casting is hopeless. Timing controls the forces that build up and subside. Such a flow of action is graceful, a beautiful thing to behold. Sudden stops and starts—herky-jerky—not only destroy the grace of the cast but the chance to hook good fish.

The caster is guided by feel, not by formula. As one motion blends into another, the feel of things comes right through the rod into the hand, wrist, and arm. Everything is coordinated to the degree that a rod in motion gives both the appearance and the feel of being an extension of the caster. Such fluidity is derived only from practice. And practice means stealing a few precious moments from each fishing session to work on or perfect a technique.

Once classic presentation becomes second nature, with appropriate modifications according to the needs of the moment, each properly negotiated cast makes anticipation more intense, satisfaction more abundant, and hooking a good trout more likely.

My Favorite Places to Fish	Type of Fish	Best Time	Suggested Flies	
			Type	Size
Penns Creek, near Weikert, South Central Pennsylvania	Brown	June	1. Sulphur 2. Quill Gordon 3. Honey Neversink Skater Fly	18 14 16
Spruce Creek and Juanita River, vicinity of mouth of Spruce Creek, South Central Pennsylvania	Brown	June	1. Sulphur * 2. Dark Hen- drickson 3. Trico	18 14 24
Yellow Breeches Creek, Boiling Springs, Pennsylvania	Brown	April and June	1. Dark Hen- drickson 2. Adams 3. Sulphur	 14 18 18
Letort, near Carlisle, Pennsylvania	Brown	All year	1. Sulphur 2. Cricket 3. Jassid	18 16 18
Little Southwest Miramichi, Northwest Miramichi, Cains River, New Brunswick, Canada	Atlantic salmon	September	1. Mitchell 2. Silver Wilkinson † 3. Neversink Skater Fly	10–14 8–12 10–16

* My favorite sulphur is tied by George Harvey of State College, Pennsylvania.
† I use Lee Wulff's riffled hitch quite a bit on wet flies, which is surface fishing.

To his intimates, Art Flick is affectionately known as "The Laird of the Westkill." To his many friends, he is known as a man with the courage to fight for his convictions and as a great fisherman. To his host of admirers, he is famous as one of the finest flytiers in the United States.

As a conservationist, he is a pioneer and a champion for clean water. He served as a president of both the Catskill Mountains Fish and Game Club and the Federated Sportsmen's Clubs of Greene County. He is a past vice-president of the New York State Conservation Council and has served on the Advisory Committee of four Conservation Commissioners in New York State.

His articles have appeared in many periodicals, and he is the author of the best-selling classic Streamside Guide to Naturals and Their Imitations. He is the editor of Art Flick's Master Fly Tying Guide.

10. How To Fish Pocket Water

Art Flick

IT HAS ALWAYS been difficult for me to understand why so many trout fishermen spend most of their fishing time in pools or fairly smooth water and so little time working pocket water. Possibly—more likely, probably—they do not realize they are missing a good bet and some mighty interesting fishing.

Over the years at least 75 percent of my fishing efforts have been devoted to fishing pocket water. Actually, the only time I spend in pools and smooth-flowing water is in the early spring when the Quill Gordons and Hendricksons are emerging or in the late evening. Since I am almost entirely a dry-fly fisherman, visibility is the deciding factor to me. A dry fly is hard to see in fast water at dusk; it is much more visible on flat water.

Admittedly, pocket-water fishing is much more work, but for several reasons it is also much more rewarding. First, the fish are less apt to be disturbed in pocket water than they are in other portions of a river. A big factor to me is that fish can be "pounded up" more readily in such water and, as a rule, will rise more readily. Obviously, pocket-water trout do not have as much time to look over a fly as they do in pools or even in less turbulent areas of a stream; if they don't take a fly, natural or otherwise, right now, it is quickly rushed downstream and lost to them. They must make up their minds in a hurry. Finally, riffles and pockets hold an abundance of aquatic insects. Many of the more important mayflies require more oxygen than is found in the slower-moving portions of a river. The nymphs of stone flies, as well as many caddis flies, are especially partial to this type of water.

At first glance, fishermen tend to assume that certain runs are too fast to harbor trout. Not so. Apparently there is no such thing as water that is too fast or too turbulent for trout. Despite the fact that I have been primarily a pocket-water fisherman for more years than I care to remember, just several years ago Charlie Brooks, a great Western fly fisherman, guide, and author (*Larger Trout for the Western Fly Fisherman, The Trout and the Stream, Nymph Fishing for Larger Trout*), showed me that large trout, both rainbows and browns, could be taken in water so turbulent that I would not normally have fished it. We tend to forget that a goodly share of the turbulence is on the surface, with much less in the deeper portions. It doesn't take much of a submerged rock to stop this heavy flow, nor does it take very long for a fish to discover such a safe lair with excellent access to food.

When fishing pools, one has to depend mainly upon hatches and feeding fish to furnish sport. If there are no fish rising, fishing such water is seldom very productive with a dry fly, although I'll be the first to admit that it is much easier to fish than fast pocket water; easier but a lot less interesting. On the other hand, when no flies are emerging, if you fish properly, it is generally possible to raise fish—often very good-sized trout—almost any time of the day in the pockets.

When I started trout fishing back in the early twenties, dry-fly fishing was practically unknown in this country; even bucktails had not been developed. If you wanted to fish artificials, you bought snelled wet flies, and when fishing pocket water—which many fishermen did in those days—the standard fare was three wet flies. The most successful fishermen fished them upstream, doing a certain amount of dapping. The flies were fished with a short leader; more often than not the line and leader

Typical pocket-water sections: 1. Riffle above pocket-water section. 2. Boulder pocket. 3. Pocket below a boulder. 4. Pocket beside a boulder. 5. Eddy pocket below or in boulders.

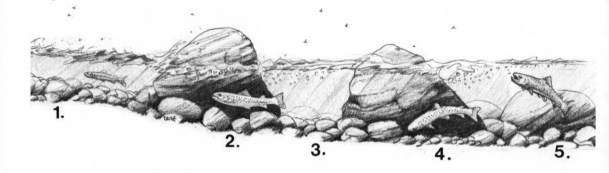

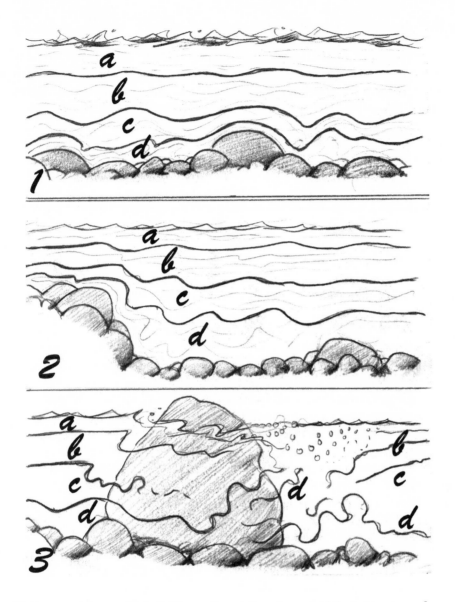

Stream current speeds: 1. Riffle, a. fastest flow, b. second fastest, c. second slowest, d. slowest to calm. 2. From riffle to pocket speeds. 3. Boulder pocket current flow and speed.

were hardly longer than the length of the rod, which in those days was a 9-footer. Tackle refinements came much later. Small bucktails, wet flies, and nymphs are still all suitable for pocket-water fishing and if fished properly, with the rod high, the fly quite near the surface, will give the same visual satisfaction as floaters. It makes little difference what you call the fly if it is fished in such a manner, upstream, and is at the surface so you can actually see the take. There are times when the fish will only take such offerings. This method can be applied to dry-fly fishing as well. I generally fish two flies in water too turbulent to float a fly; one a sparsely tied type for the tail and a more heavily hackled one for the dropper. The casts are short, with the rod held high and the dropper fly being kept on the surface almost all the time, as in dapping. In fact, it is dapping at its best, and when fish take, they really smash the fly. This type of fishing obviously works better on feeder streams.

But I vastly prefer dry-fly fishing whenever I can get it. When one starts fishing pocket water with a dry fly, it may seem more difficult—and it probably is—until you get the knack of it. Like everything else in fishing the floater, it takes some doing.

Actually, I get more satisfaction from pounding up a fish in such water—one that isn't showing—than I do from catching a rising fish. The toughest part of dry-fly fishing in pockets is to avoid drag. But where drag may startle a fish in pools or smoother water, it doesn't seem to do so in fast water, as long as you leave the fly until ready for the pickup. Don't attempt to take the fly from the water until it has passed the area you are interested in fishing. Usually a 9-foot leader will suffice, but I like one that is 12 feet long, which I think gives me a slightly longer dragfree float. Any place that will float a fly, if only for a few feet, should be fished. Visibility in this type of fishing is not quite so important, because most of the rises will be the splashy kind and will be readily seen. Pocket-water trout don't sip or glide up toward a fly to get it coming down in fast water.

Sometimes you can avoid drag by raising your arm immediately after making the cast, thereby removing your line from the stream surface so that only a portion of the leader is on the surface, which explains why the longer leader is valuable. With a bit of practice this will enable you to get a bit longer dragfree float. Another trick that works well under certain conditions is to make your cast across a rock, so that a portion of your line is on the rock instead of on the stream surface.

Very often there are slow-moving glides along the edges of the stream, while the center portion is turbulent. Be sure to fish such areas carefully, making your first cast to the lower portion so that you don't "line a fish." On this first cast, unless you are fortunate, you will only get a very short dragfree float. Be sure to leave the fly on the water and not pick it up until it is past the tail of the glide; otherwise all you will see will be the wake of a fish—a frightened one at that. Often I have found larger trout in such areas, but they are tough places to fish.

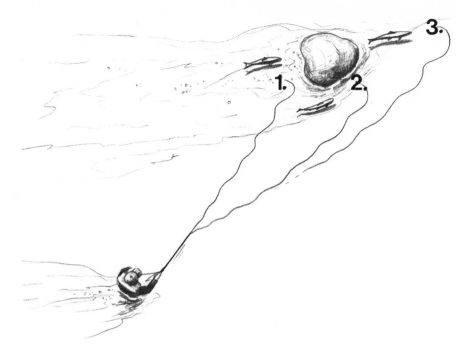

Boulder pockets: 1. Behind boulder; the slowest water pocket. 2. Beside boulder; slow. Also food-gathering area. 3. In front of boulder—depression pocket.

Where a boulder forms a pocket, affording a comparatively still piece of water, again be sure to fish the lower bit of the still water first; often a good trout will be found there. In taking up such a position, a trout can see food being washed down on either side of the boulder. After the more still portion is fished, work both sides of the pocket, fishing the side with the slower flow the hardest; then carefully fish just ahead of the boulder. The water will often be flowing faster on the surface ahead of the boulder, for the chances are that this same boulder has formed a slight depression ahead of it, making a fine lay for a trout. I try not to miss any of such water, because trout will come up out of surprising lies. Although it may not be visible to you, there may be an undercut bank or root along the bank; both make wonderful hiding places for trout.

Most of this fishing is done with a comparatively short cast. The rod should be held high, giving you complete control of your flies, and you should work them in every available run. It is these runs that bring food down to the fish. Try to float your fly down at the same speed as the current, and remember to fish a high rod.

The best flies to use for such water are bushy, high-floating flies

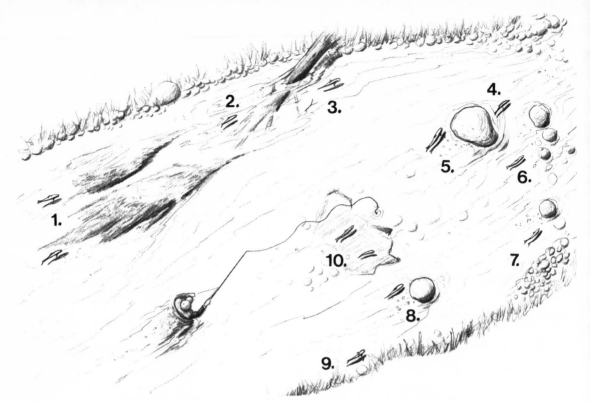

Overhead view of large-stream pocket-water areas: 1. Below moss beds. 2. Behind logs or fallen trees. 3. Above deadfalls. 4. In front of surface boulder. 5. Behind or below surface boulder. 6. Below fast-riffle rubbles. 7. In water breaking over gravel bar. 8. Beside and behind boulder in slower water. 9. Along edges of stream. 10. In bedrock faults.

such as the variants, the Wulffs, and even the old-type bivisibles. All float higher and better and can be more easily seen by you and the trout than conventional patterns. Such patterns tied on size 14 hooks do well. I personally fish properly tied variants—the Gray Fox and Dun—about 95 percent of the time and rarely see any need to use flotant, except after I have removed a fly from a fish.

You will find that you get many takes even when the most buoyant fly has slipped beneath the surface, which makes pocket-water fishing quite different from other types of dry-fly fishing. Don't take your eye off the fly for even a second, because that is about the length of time it takes a fish to grab it. If you don't see some sign of the take, you have given it an advantage—one it doesn't need.

The best part of this type of fishing is that you can often get some action when there are no flies emerging. Obviously, if flies were coming, you would be in water that was easier to fish, where feeding trout could be spotted more readily. Save the pocket water for times when

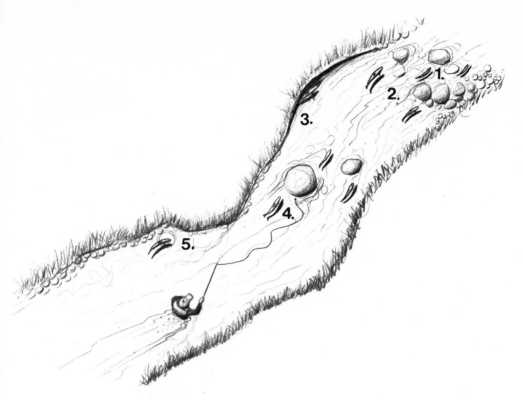

Overhead view of small-stream sections of pocket water: 1. Riffle pockets. 2. Drop-off pocket below riffle. 3. Undercut-bank pocket. 4. Pockets above and below midstream exposed boulder. 5. Bank-eddy pocket.

there is no visible activity and flies are not emerging. Time seems to pass more quickly when you fish pocket water, and if you have some weighty problem gnawing at you that you want to get away from, then go to such water; you won't have time to think of anything but the business at hand. This is fast, concentrated fishing. There isn't time to gawk around as you might do when fishing pools or slow-moving water; in fast water you must keep your eye riveted to the fly.

Wading such water can be a bit tricky. If you're careless, it is easy to wind up with a bath. As often as not, you simply cannot see for sure where you are putting your foot. You must be certain not to lift your rear foot until your forward foot is firmly settled. This may sound like foolish advice. However, if one is moving forward and puts a foot down on what he thinks is firm footing but which isn't, when he picks up his other foot, there is an immediate loss of balance. This, combined with the relentless action of the current, usually means a wet fanny. And it can happen in a big hurry.

When you fish pocket water regularly, reading the water will come naturally. You will soon learn the kind of situation in which you can expect to find a fish, and the knowledge gained will, of course, apply to many other areas. Each time you raise a trout make a mental note of the type of water it is, and be on the lookout for such a setup in the future. You will be amazed at how often fish can be found in similar spots. Little by little you will have a mental catalog of where you may expect to find them.

It is very important to read the water in a stretch of stream you do not know well. Where visibility permits, study the bottom with special care to try to ascertain if there are any boulders that are even slightly higher than the rest of the stream bottom. If so, the chances are good that this will be a place where trout can be found, since the rock will break the force of the water. Also bear in mind that trout, when not on the feed, are often resting close to the bottom, where there is considerably less force in the current. Any portion of the stream that appears to be boiling is worth your efforts. Boiling is caused by the force of the current against submerged rocks; these areas very often hold good fish. If you learn to read water in one stream, it is likely that the lessons learned will apply to almost any stretch of pocket water on any given stream.

I recall well a trip I took to a stream owned by a famous fly-fishing club. It was a bright day in mid-June, when most of the daytime hatches had come and gone, so I had little, if any, hope of seeing fish work, except possibly to a terrestrial now and then. I had never fished the water before and was anxious to try it, but I was told not to expect much action until evening on such a bright day.

Some members very graciously showed me a few of the pools, which were quite lovely. By approaching carefully, we could see many trout, some of them really good fish. Because most of the club members

Ledge-rock pocket.

were older men, I was quite certain these pools got the brunt of the fishing.

After a delicious lunch, my friends invited me to try my luck, but they doubted that there would be much action until the sun got off the water. I'd seen some very interesting pocket water and runs that might very well hold good trout, so I decided to start out early in the afternoon.

Luck was with me. It seemed as though those fish had rarely, if ever, seen an artificial fly. Admittedly, I fished the stretches I thought were the least likely to be fished by the members, but I had a field day. These faster stretches, unlike the pools, had not been as heavily stocked, and trout were less numerous. This made for some very interesting fishing, as did the fact that these fast stretches held good numbers of wild fish.

On my return to the club, when queried as to how I'd done, I was not ashamed to show four browns—the club limit, which I had been told I could keep—the smallest a shade larger than 14 inches. They all allowed they would be damned: fish like *that* on a bright June afternoon!

I'm reasonably sure that some of that fast water has been fished since.

Obviously, you are not going to strike it so rich on public water, but you can be reasonably certain that you'll get better action anywhere on the more oxygenated portions of a stream, even when no fish are showing. Isn't it reasonable to assume that fish in the more turbulent areas of a river require more food? This, combined with the fact that food is harder to come by, gives the angler a much better chance.

Presentation, as in any fishing with a dry fly, is all-important. However, in pocket water an angler can make more mistakes and get away with them than on slow-moving or glassy sections and pools.

Submerged rocks form pockets; boiling water indicates their power.

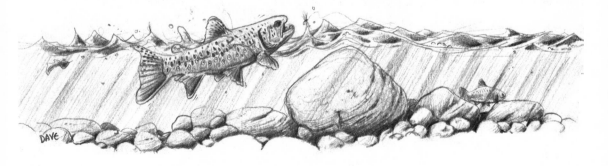

Finally, your fishing opportunities may be limited, and you might think yourself unfortunate enough on one of them to run into a warm, bright afternoon when it seems useless to fish. Don't believe it. Instead of giving up most of the day waiting for the cooler evening fishing, take a trip to a feeder stream that will very likely consist of pocket water—or to a section of your favorite river where the water runs fast. If the section is well shaded, so much the better, and if the water temperature is below 70 degrees, you may be pleasantly surprised. Even though the water is in the high 60s, the fact that it is pocket water means that it will have more oxygen, giving you at least a decent chance at some sport.

Pocket-water fishing is fast and often exciting. It requires a quick eye and quick reflexes. It demands your utmost attention. But it can often be the most productive sport you'll find on any trout stream. It is far too often neglected.

My Favorite Places to Fish	Type of Fish	Best Time	Suggested Flies Type	Size
Delaware River, Delaware County, Lordville, New York	Rainbow Brown	Depends on flow	1. Variants 2. Hendrickson 3. Adams	14 12 12
East Branch of Delaware River, Delaware County, New York	Brown	Depends on flow	1. Hendrickson 2. Variants 3. Adams	12 14 12
Esopus Creek, Ulster County, New York	Rainbow Brown	Spring	1. Quill Gordon 2. Hendrickson 3. Variants	14 12 12
Schoharie River, Greene County, New York	Brown	Spring September if water is up	1. Quill Gordon 2. Hendrickson 3. Variants	14 12 12
Batten Kill, downstream from Vermont line, New York	Brown Brook	Spring September	1. Hendrickson 2. Adams 3. Trycorithodes	12 12 18–20

Ernest Schwiebert caught his first trout in a Michigan creek at the age of five. Since then he has fished the dry fly from Tierra del Fuego to Labrador, and from Alaska and Lapland to the Antipodes.

He is a well-known architect and planner, with degrees from Ohio State and Princeton, where he completed his doctorate in 1966.

Besides being one of the top anglers, he has also achieved fame as a writer. His articles have appeared in Sports Illustrated, Life, Esquire, True, Field & Stream, Atlantic, The Fly Fisherman, *and* Sports Afield, *where he serves as a contributing editor.*

His books include Matching the Hatch, *a portfolio of paintings titled* Salmon of the World, *the best-selling* Nymphs, *a collection of stories called* Remembrances of Rivers Past, *and the huge two-volume* Trout.

11. Special Presentations
Downstream, the Dump Cast,
and the Twitch

Ernest Schwiebert

CHILBOLTON-ON-TEST lies a few miles upstream from Stock-
bridge, where members of the Houghton Club have stayed at the Gros-
venor Arms since 1822. The Chronicles of that fishing membership have
existed without interruption since that time, and its rolls have included
many famous fishing writers. Canon Charles Kingsley recorded his experiences on the Houghton water in his charming *Chalkstream Studies*
of 1857, and Francis Francis was writing about the Test in those same
years. George Selwyn Marryat and Frederic Halford fished it regularly
twenty-odd years later, and although the dry-fly method apparently
evolved on the neighboring Itchen and Wandle, Captain Marryat and
Halford unquestionably refined and codified its philosophy at Stock-
bridge.

Other famous anglers also populate the history of the Test. Izaak
Walton himself lived out his twilight years there at his Norington farm-
stead, near a place called Watership Down, and purportedly carved the
mantelpiece at Testcombe House.

Our century has produced its chalk-stream heroes too. John Waller
Hills retired to fish at Mottisfont and produced classics like *A History of
Fly Fishing for Trout* and his lyric book called *A Summer on the Test.*
Colonel E. W. Harding and J. W. Dunne followed in his footsteps.
Harding produced a brilliant theoretical book titled *The Flyfisher and
the Trout's Point of View*, and Dunne worked out the theories in his
Sunshine and the Dry Fly at Longparish. Dermot Wilson lives in a
refurbished mill at Nether Wallop and is perhaps the dean of the Test in
our time.

Wilson served as my host for a week of fishing on his lower beats at Kimbridge, below the Houghton Club mileage, and on the upper river at Longparish and Chilbolton-on-Test. It was a fascinating walk with ghosts, and my favorite water was at Testcombe House on the beats that Richard Durnford fished more than one hundred fifty years ago.

It was during a morning hatch of pale wateries that I had my baptism at Testcombe and became fully aware of the almost religious dogma that echoes from the Halford years. It has been exactly a century since Halford published his *Floating Flies and How to Dress Them*, yet its rigid philosophical code still imprisons fishing theory on the chalk streams.

"The fishing rules we observe are strict and traditional at Testcombe." Dermot Wilson lit another woodbine at the fishing cottage. "You must not fish downstream."

"Even with dry flies?" I asked.

"That's right," Wilson cautioned, "and particularly with wet flies and nymphs. And no bucktails either."

"Pretty austere code." I smiled.

The dry-fly code evolved by Marryat and Halford still lives on the Test, from Broadlands and Romsey on the lower river to the headwaters above Whitchurch and Hurstbourne Priors, where its currents are joined by the lyric Bourne.

The Halford code was quite rigid and unforgiving. All casts should be delivered upstream or quartering across stream, and all techniques were focused on achieving a dragfree float. His philosophy was primarily concerned with imitating the prolific hatches of mayflies on the Test, although his fly-dressing chapters in *Floating Flies and How to Dress Them* include both mayfly-style uprights and the typical downwing sedge characteristic of British flymakers.

During my first morning at Testcombe, with Dermot Wilson and Capt. Jack Sheppard, the fish worked daintily on a mixed hatch of medium olives and pale watery duns. It was a summery, wine-aired day in Hampshire, and the trout performed like the chalk stream fish in all the books I had read over the years.

We walked the grassy banks with a mixture of laziness and stealth, watching for the dimpling rings and bulges against the weeds that betrayed a rising fish. It was a leisurely pace, totally unlike the restless searching of the water at random that seems to suit the American temperament. Yet our rivers are hard-fished these days, and random casting can often line a trout and put him down. The patient searching casts of Emlyn Gill and George La Branche are less effective in our time, except in tumbling rivers filled with less demanding trout. Accomplished fishermen from the Housatonic in Connecticut to Hat Creek in California have discovered that patient observation is the secret and that their casting should be limited to rising fish.

However, it seems proper to confess that I took my best trout at Chilbolton-on-Test with a downstream dry fly. The fish went 3 pounds and was lying under the upstream frame of a weed-rack. It obviously understood the rules that prohibited casting downstream, since it was impossible to catch by casting upstream or across. And fishing downstream, there would only be one workable float.

The first cast was rejected when the trout took a natural an inch from my fly. My reflex took the fly away, and the frightened fish stopped rising. It was time to let the trout forget, and I walked upstream to try another. The second time I tried the weed-rack fish my fly was rejected and became fouled in the frame. Trying to roll cast it free would alarm the trout, so I pointed the rod at the fly and broke the tippet.

The trout seemingly sensed the imperceptible vibration transmitted into the weed-rack and stopped feeding. Damn! I thought. Wonder if he'll start working again.

Forty-five minutes later I walked back down the water meadow and found the weed-rack trout rising. It had taken up a new feeding station about four feet closer to my bank, although it was still a difficult cast of sixty feet.

My third attempt fell slightly off target when I checked the downstream cast, and the fly dropped a few inches beyond the trout's feeding lane. I shook another two feet of line into the float with a waggling of the rod tip, and when the tiny medium olive drifted close, the fish turned to its left and inhaled it.

The weed-rack was hazardous, but the trout made a mistake when it felt me tighten. It bolted upstream instead of turning under the frame to safety, and a gentle side pressure coaxed it away from its haven. It finally surrendered to my net, and I released it gently in the quiet shallows.

"That downstream cast is our secret," I whispered.

Halford and Marryat would have considered my downstream presentation an unacceptable heresy, yet skilled American anglers are turning more and more to a downstream float over selective fish. Many of our finest trout streams have been designated catch-and-release fisheries, restricted to fly fishing only. Trout that have been caught and released several times become surprisingly tippet-shy, and upstream casts consistently spook them, however skillful the hook casts that are thrown.

Another heresy that would offend the Halford code is the grasshop-

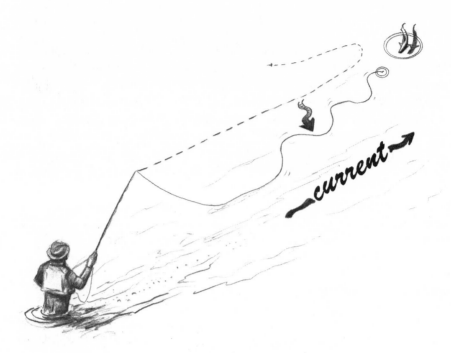

Downstream cast.

per or bump cast. Marryat was famous for the precision and delicacy of his dry-fly presentation, delivering his fragile uprights like thistledown. Halford revered his mentor for his exquisite casting and would have found a cast offensive that intentionally dropped the fly on the water hard.

Colonel Harding was perhaps first to observe, in his classic *Fly-fisher and the Trout's Point of View*, that not all insects fall softly into the current. Mating damselflies and big drakes often lay their eggs with surprising impact in the surface film. Many terrestrials also fall into the water clumsily, particularly large carpenter ants, grasshoppers, gypsy moth larvae, inchworms, leafrollers, beetles, and even the tiny leafhoppers. Trout often lie watching the surface film, waiting for the delicate explosion of lights that betray a hapless terrestrial.

Trout frequently range widely about a shallow flat, taking insects that clearly fall far outside their circle of vision. There have been many experiences with the bump-cast technique in grasshopper time, particularly on Silver Creek in Idaho and in the Geyser Meadows along the firehole in the Yellowstone.

There was a heavy brown below the mouth of Sentinel Creek that was typical. It was lying under the grass, holding in the cool flow of the creek that eddies along the bank. The cast failed to turn over with an unexpected gust of wind, dumping my grasshopper five feet from the grass and a full ten feet below the fish. The trout left its station with a vicious swirl and took the fly savagely, pushing a heartstopping bow wake as it came.

There's no way the fish could have seen that fly, I thought, but he sure saw it hit the water!

Two incidents on the Brodhead in Pennsylvania are indelible in my mind. The first took place on the Buttonwood pool in leafroller time, when the sycamores were filled with the bright green larvae dangling on their silken threads. The second took place at the Pine Tree pool, during an early summer infestation of gypsy moth larvae in the oaks and maples.

The Buttonwood pool was alive with trout lying in wait for the leafrollers to fall into the water. It was a perfect afternoon to have an in-experienced fisherman on the Brodhead, because its trout are shy and selective. The rises were bold and showy as the fish stalked the helpless leafrollers that either fell into the pool or dragged in the surface film on their threads. The trout were so greedy that even bad casts and dragging flies seemed to attract their attention at surprising distances. The beginner with me that day took six good trout in spite of his casting and his dragging floats, breaking off a fish that must have measured 20 inches. That trout came almost thirty feet to take a leafroller with a poor cast that dropped the fly hard in the shallows, well off target.

Cooperative fish! I thought. He sure wanted that fly!

Bump cast.

Those Buttonwood trout were remarkable examples of fish that came to the impact point of flies cast far outside their circles of vision, but the Pine Tree example is still more dramatic.

Gypsy moth larvae were devouring the new leaves in the hardwoods that sheltered the pool, and two fish were lying in the tail shallows. The trout were about twenty feet apart, and I decided to try the lower fish first. But the cast came down awkwardly, spooking the fish when the leader splashed. Before I could pick up for another cast, the second fish bolted downstream, took the fly almost angrily, and hooked itself. Since my fly fell directly below the trout, in the blind angle behind its head, it was impossible for the fish to see the fly or its impact on the surface.

Must have heard it land! I shook my head.

Both Skues and Colonel Harding observed in their writings that Halford's philosophy of the dragless float lacked infallibility, and that some aquatic insects often scuttled across the surface or hopscotched down the current, laying their eggs. Edward Ringwood Hewitt developed his famous skater dry flies on his Neversink holdings and described their use in his book *A Trout and Salmon Fisherman for Seventy-five Years*. His skaters were long-hackled flies dressed on tiny light-wire hooks and were fished with a skittering, fluttering retrieve across the surface of his Neversink flats.

John Waller Hills wrote *Riverkeeper*, the biography of William Lunn, and in its pages describes fishing the Caperer at the Houghton Club. The Caperer is a brownish traveling sedge, imitated with a mottled down-wing dry fly, and Hills's pattern was fished with a twitching drift designed to induce a rise. Hills also confesses, in his *Summer on the Test*, that the Caperer was his favorite fly pattern through the summer months.

Roger Foster is a highly skilled riverkeeper on the Maigue in southern Ireland and is justly famous for his induced-rise tactics in sedge season. Several years ago we were fishing his lush water meadows at Dunraven Castle.

It is some of the loveliest dry-fly water anywhere, rich with fly life and ranunculus, its fertility born of limestone springs in the rolling, foxhunting country below Limerick. The castle beats are shrouded in history, with the ruins of a tenth-century fortress and the broken nave of a twelfth-century abbey upstream. The Maigue is a remarkable brown-trout fishery, its selective fish averaging a pound or better, and there are few rivers with more prolific fly hatches.

I had hoped to find good hatches of *Ephemera vulgata*, the big green drakes indigenous to the rivers and lakes of Ireland, but we were a week too early. Only a few mayflies were hatching sporadically on the Maigue, and the trout were not taking them yet.

"They're not on the mayfly yet," Foster explained, "but on rainy days we've got iron blues and lots of sedges!"

"Sounds good," I said.

Foster was right about the sedges. There were so many caddis flies in the weeds and bank grasses that I gathered them like berries for my collecting bottle. The killing jar was quickly filled with dark little silverhorns, *Sericostoma* flies, and cinnamon sedges.

On the first evening we walked down to the Maigue where it wound out from the trees into the water meadows below the castle. The twilight was alive with sedges. Fish were working everywhere, in the swift currents below the weirs and undercut banks in the shamrock-filled meadows downstream.

"They're on the sedges," Foster said.

"We've seen several kinds of caddis flies." I grinned. "How do we know which one they're taking?"

"Silverhorns hatch mainly at night," Foster explained, "and the Welshman's buttons are almost finished."

"And that leaves the cinnamon sedges," I said.

"You're learning." Foster smiled.

His Wheatley boxes were filled with elegant little sedges, and I clinched one to my tippet. There were several refusal swirls under my fly and a few halfhearted rises, but I failed to hook a fish. The riverkeeper was fishing downstream, and I watched him take a fat 15-inch brown. Foster released the trout and promptly hooked another just above the weir. Two more fish swirled under my fly, and when a third missed it splashily, I walked downstream to watch Foster fish his sedge.

"My tactics aren't working," I said.

Foster was carefully preening his fly. "I'm fishing it with the induced-rise technique," he explained.

"And it teases them into taking?" I asked.

"It works," Foster said, nodding.

Foster demonstrated over another fish. His line worked out and dropped the fly above the fish's feeding station, and the sedge settled about a foot above the fish. The little sedge had scarcely started its float when Foster gave it a subtle twitch, let it float another six inches, and teased it again. It was too much for the trout, and it took the fly hard.

"So that's your induced-rise method," I said.

"Yes." The riverkeeper nodded. "Sometimes it coaxes a sedging fish into taking the fly."

In the years since Skues and Harding and Lunn, such methods

have become widespread. Leonard Wright is a skilled flyfisher who works his home waters in the Catskills, and in books such as *Fishing the Dry Fly as a Living Insect* and *Fly-fishing Heresies*, Wright has firmly demonstrated his opposition to the ex cathedra arguments that permeate much of this sport. American anglers, unfamiliar with the induced-rise tactics found on the famous streams of England and Ireland, found Wright's *Fishing the Dry Fly* a revelation, with its advocacy of downstream casts and controlled drag. Yet such tactics clearly suggest the behavior of the prolific caddis flies.

Perhaps the most difficult fishing in the United States is found in the Harriman Flats on the Henrys Fork in Idaho. It is a large river, two hundred to three hundred yards wide and waist deep, with an easy bottom. Rich beds of aquatic vegetation undulate lazily in its smooth currents, and both its weeds and its fly hatches echo its astonishing fertility.

Since trout are caught and released on this 10-mile stretch of water for fly fishing only, and big hatches are almost continuous through the summer months, the fish become remarkably tippet-shy and selective. Downstream presentation is common. Sixteen- to twenty-foot leaders are the rule, and tippets range from .005 and .003, depending on the skill of the fisherman. Many knowledgeable anglers on the Henrys Fork add a 36-inch tippet to their bag of tricks, using its flexibility to get a dragfree float.

This past spring on the Henrys Fork, with fifty trumpeter swans nesting on the lake at the Harriman Ranch and the water meadows purple with lupine, we had exceptional fishing below Last Chance. It was a spring of eagles fishing from their jackstraw nesting in trees below the ranch and its outbuildings, and surprising hatches of big, slate-winged *Ephemereus* flies in the meadows above Millionaire's Flat.

It was the prelude to a special summer when Dan Callaghan and I joined Jack Hemingway and his half-brothers, Patrick and Gregory, on the Henrys Fork. Patrick was an exile from Africa, returned from the eroding fortunes of big-game hunting and his efforts at teaching conservation in Kenya, and had come down with Gregory from Montana for the fine early hatches. Gregory had just published a book entitled *Papa*, his rememberances of life with their father, and it was the first time the three Hemingway sons had been together since their father's funeral at Sun Valley.

Big slate-winged olives were already hatching when we reached the river, and Jack Hemingway promptly hooked a heavy rainbow on a dry fly. The fish bored wildly across the river, jumped twice, and was gone in its second cartwheel. It was the only good fish we found taking the big mayflies.

Induced-rise method.

The whitefish took them greedily with splashy rises, but only the smaller trout, gullible fish of 12 to 16 inches, took the olive-bodied drakes while they lasted. The bigger rainbows scorned them with inspection rises, their noses virtually touching the big hopscotching mayflies with a mixture of caution and disbelief, and took only the smaller flies that were hatching.

"They're a little shy," Jack Hemingway shouted downstream. "They act like they can't believe these drakes!"

Beyond the weeds along the marshy island, two big rainbows lazily sipped a hatch of tiny, two-tailed duns. The larger fish ignored the big, olive-bodied drakes entirely, but the smaller trout tipped up halfheartedly to study them. The flies were fluttering awkwardly down the current, their lead-colored wings drying slowly in the cool wind, and the smaller fish was curious.

It had been feeding on tiny olives and pale-bodied duns for several weeks, and these big drakes were puzzling. It drifted back under each struggling drake that came down its feeding lane, but it was wary and suspicious. Several times it floated six to ten feet downstream, watching a clumsy drake free itself from its nymphal shuck and hopscotch on the current.

Each time the big rainbow studied the struggling mayfly, poised to

take it greedily, and each time it had second thoughts. It sank back war-
ily and returned to its feeding station.

"They're too big and too dark!" I watched with amazement. "He's
been taking tiny flies for several weeks, and he's afraid of these big,
green-bodied drakes!"

"You're right," Dan Callaghan agreed. "That fish thinks nothing
that big is safe, and he lets the big drakes go!"

The pattern was inflexible, although both rainbows took a smaller,
straw-colored mayfly steadily. Finally I hooked the larger fish on a delicate pale morning dun, and it threshed angrily when I tightened, shooting a hundred feet upstream before it jumped in a spray-scattering
cartwheel.

The straining tippet held, singing with the tension as it sliced the
current and raked sickeningly across the weeds. Twice it caught and
held briefly and twice it came free. The fight settled quickly into stub-
born infighting, burrowing under weed beds, and circling in the shallows, but finally the fish surrendered and I netted it gratefully.

"How big?" Callaghan shouted.

"He's a good fish," I yelled back. "He's strong and deep, and he'll
go 4 pounds—maybe a little more."

"Let's celebrate with some lunch," Callaghan said.

We released the big rainbow in a quiet current tongue between the
weeds and walked up through the lupine and Indian paintbrush. Lunch
on the tailgate of the Peugeot was roast chicken and richly spiced salami,
with a quiche from the Hemingway kitchen and a river-chilled bottle of
Sancerre.

There were stories of the morning's sport mixed with echoes of
Africa and Key West summers and mornings at the Finca Vigia outside
Havana in their boyhood years, when their father was writing well and
the sport was good. There was laughter about those years and the popular Hemingway mythologies that still travel the literary world. There
were also unspoken exchanges between men who had witnessed the
somber, melancholy years when their father's quicksilver talent began to
wither and go sour.

The river sparkled in the sun, running swiftly in its weedy channels
above the ranch buildings in the trees, and we lay happily in the wild-
flowers, listening to the mating curlews and sandhill cranes and waiting
for the evening rise.

Two eagles were circling Millionaire's Flat when we rigged our
equipment and walked downstream. There was fresh snow on the Te-
tons, their escarpment startlingly highlighted on the horizon, and a few
fish were working on sedges.

Jack Hemingway selected a slate-colored sedge from his chest box. It was dressed with dark blue dun hackles and wings of mallard primary-sections tied down over a dull olive dubbing.

"That's a good-looking fly," I said.

"Rene Harrop ties them for me in Saint Anthony," Hemingway explained. "The Henrys Fork fish seem to like them."

"Could I try one?" I asked.

Hemingway fished another tiny sedge from his box, and I hooked it lightly into my sweater while I replaced the .003 tippet I had been using that morning. That big rainbow used up all its stretch, I thought. Better start fresh!

When the 36-inch tippet was ready, I retrieved the tiny sedge and clinch-knotted it to the nylon. Hemingway was already stalking a big fish in the bend the Henrys Fork regulars call Battleship Row, and I slipped quietly into the river. Since the best fish often lie tight against its undercut banks, working softly against the trailing grass, the best tactic involves wading and watching both banks with a mixture of patience and stealth. Skilled Henrys Fork fishermen are like herons and can cover less than fifty yards of water in several hours.

Finally I located a sucking dimple tight against the bank that looked good and I waded carefully into range. The rise was soft, but its after-rise disturbance bulged and flowed against the bank grasses.

Good fish! I thought excitedly.

My first cast worked slightly upstream and settled softly against the bank, but the line bellied quickly and a slight drag disturbed the quiet eddy where the fish was lying. Just when I was afraid that the trout had

been alarmed by the dragging fly, it bulged again along the weeds. Several slack-line casts and left hooks failed to achieve a workable float, so I moved slightly upstream to cast directly across the current tongue.

There was still a teasing little drag in spite of my slack casts and mends, and I finally eased into position for a quartering dry-fly cast downstream. "Let's try you again with a change of angle," I thought aloud.

The cast worked out softly, and I checked it to throw some gentle loops of slack. The fly settled six inches above the trout, floated perfectly, and was refused.

I let the fly drift on through the fish until it had passed well below the fish's station. The trout took a tiny fluttering sedge just as I picked up the fly, and suddenly it took another. Try an induced-rise float, I thought, and twitch the fly.

The tiny sedge floated six inches down the feeding lane against the grass, and as it reached the trout I twitched it a half inch. The big rainbow took it solidly.

My reel protested shrilly, as the fish bolted a hundred yards down Millionaire's Flat and jumped in front of Hemingway. "Your fish has terrible manners!" His booming laughter echoed upriver. "He's jumping in my water!"

The big rainbow was running again, although I had regained some line between jumps, and I held the rod high above my head to keep the weed from shearing my tippet. After the first few jumps, it was a long fight on fine gear, with the fish circling me endlessly thirty yards out.

Finally it surrendered. It measured just over 23 inches in the net, and I coaxed it carefully back to life until I could no longer hold it in the meshes. The big fish held briefly in a weedy channel and then melted into the current.

"Good fish!" Hemingway stated.

"Broke all the rules," I answered. "He took your little sedge fished downstream with a twitch!"

"Fishing down and dragging the fly!" Hemingway laughed. "He sure hadn't read his Halford!"

"Halford would turn in his grave," I said.

My Favorite Places to Fish	*Type of Fish*	*Best Time*	*Suggested Flies* Type	*Size*
Henrys Fork of the Snake River, Last Chance, Idaho	McCloud Rainbow	June 15– July 15 August 25– September 30	1. Gray/Yellow 2. Adams 3. Sooty Olive Sedge	14–20 18–26 16–22
Firehole River, Yellowstone National Park, Montana	Rainbow	June 15– July 15 September 1– October 31	1. Gray/Yellow 2. Adams 3. Sooty Olive Sedge	14–20 16–24 16–22
Silver Creek, Sun Valley, Idaho	McCloud Rainbow	August 25– October 31	1. Gray/Yellow 2. Specklewing Spinner 3. White/Black	16–20 16–18 24–26
Au Sable River, Grayling, Michigan	Brook Brown Rainbow	May 1–15	1. White-Brown Spinner 2. Hendrickson 3. Blue Quill 4. Red Quill	12–18 12–16 18–22 14–18
Brodheads Creek, Analomink, Pennsylvania	Brown	April 15– June 15	1. Gordon Quill 2. Red Quill 3. Hendrickson	14–18 14–20 14–16

CHRISTINE FONG

Michael Fong is a native of California who earned his Master of Arts degree at the University of Iowa. Back in California, he and his wife, Christine, have become famous photographers of the fishing scene, through patience and observation.

As a fisherman, Fong has angled extensively throughout the West, including Alaska and British Columbia. He is a field tester for the Garcia Corporation.

As a conservationist, he is an active member of California Trout, Nature Conservancy, and the Federation of Fly Fishermen.

As a writer, he has been published in leading outdoor periodicals and wildlife journals and is a contributing editor of Angler Magazine.

12. Big Water
Special Techniques

Michael Fong

DEPENDING ON THE WEATHER, the seasons, and the river itself, fishing the dry fly on big water will run the gamut from slow currents to savage flows, from easy takes to demanding fishing, but always
it is fun. Enterprising anglers now recognize that the larger rivers offer a
great challenge with compensating rewards—big fish, sometimes hard
fights against tough water, and occasionally new species. The dry fly on
big water is a new and exciting adventure in fly fishing.

Fishing big water is nearly the same as fishing more intimate waters
except that almost everything is on a larger scale. The basic skills of
wading, reading water, and casting must be adapted to this larger water.
Cleated or felt-soled sandals are often a necessity, a wading staff can be
helpful, rods should be longer and more powerful, flies are often larger
(but not always) and they are usually dressed with buoyant material to
make them better floaters. On rivers where wading is not possible, the
ability to maneuver a craft—whether pram, canoe, or larger boat—can
be a distinct advantage.

For the wading angler the development of the carbon rod has been
a tremendous asset for fishing big water. With its inherent strength and
lightness, rods of longer length than ordinary have become a pleasure to
use. For trout, this greater leverage combined with the very high degree of resiliency enables casters to produce greater line speed with relatively lightweight lines, which are generally preferred for subtle presentations. Where once a rod of 7½ or 8 feet of glass or cane mated to a
weight-forward No. 5 line began to act hesitantly with a heavily dressed
size 12 fly, a 9-footer of graphite, using the identical line, can handle a

bushy size 8 fly without strain; it will still be capable of presenting a size 20 fly on a 14-foot leader with great delicacy. This flexibility is one of the main reasons why graphite is becoming more widely used by experienced big-water anglers.

The advantages of the carbon rod become especially obvious on big rivers when winds arise; they enable the fisherman to make long casts into difficult lies.

The epitome of the quiet big river, where small dries are practical, is Idaho's Henrys Fork of the Snake River. For most of the summer the stock hatches on that section bordered by the Railroad Ranch include mayflies in sizes smaller than 20—to about 16. Despite their size, these diminutive flies consistently bring good trout to the top.

As with most smooth-flowing rivers, taking large fish is heavily dependent upon approach. All else being equal, the angler who can pick out the most likely takers or holds will end up with the most action. If the fish have eyeballed many artificials and have even been fooled a time or two, then the art of presentation will play a more important role, and exact imitation may become a must. If I had only one cast on which to place my best hopes on waters like the Henrys Fork or the Fall River in California, I would choose the serpentine cast, quartering downstream. The main advantages of this presentation are the length of dragfree drift and the fact that the fly will come into the view of the fish before the line. Most expert anglers agree, however, that at the moment any fish becomes vulnerable, the ability to react swiftly with whatever special cast is appropriate to that particular situation will be what takes fish.

On some big rivers that produce quality fishing, execution is not nearly as important as *when* one fishes. One of the best examples of this type of timing occurs on the Williamson River in southern Oregon. Above the junction of the Sprague River at Chiloquin, upstream to where Spring Creek enters, the Williamson is still big water; during the fall in certain years, this section holds a special treat for dry-fly fishermen.

The Williamson empties into Klamath Lake, a large body of water famed for the size and numbers of its rainbows. In the fall, depending upon how early cold weather sets in, these rainbows leave the lake and begin their ascent up the river. In those years when a prolonged freeze occurs in late September, mid-October will find some of these rainbows in the upper river; once there, they become avid takers of the substantial fall hatches of small mayflies. Since the Oregon trout season closes at the end of October, when the freeze comes late, the fish arrive after the river is closed to fishing. Although the resident rainbows can provide some interesting sport, the fishery is far better when augmented by the migrants.

If weather permits, there are two main periods of hatch activity. On most days the morning action starts at about nine thirty and lasts until noon; the evening rise is on for the two hours before dark. During both these periods the fish are generally active on the surface, but during the last hour of the day a big rainbow can sometimes startle you with its bold lack of sophistication.

Near dusk one evening I was positioned waist-deep opposite a particularly productive run. After having landed and released a nice fish, I began to use a piece of amadou to dry the fly before redressing it. Suddenly, I heard a loud slurp behind me. Without shifting my feet, I glanced around just in time to see a big rainbow take a natural in the bubbling wake caused by my waders damming the current. My fly was ready now, so I flicked out a downstream cast, nearly all leader. The fish had it immediately. I laughed to myself and thought about all the times I'd had to stalk and sneak just to make a proper presentation. Such cooperation from a fine rainbow is one of the mysteries that, for me, adds much flavor to the game.

The lower Truckee in the central Sierras of California is an especially good example of the typical big Western river. After leaving Lake Tahoe, its source, the Truckee swells as many tributaries add to its size. By the time the Little Truckee joins it at Hirshdale, the river is about as large as it gets before diversions such as irrigation ditches start to drain its stature. Local people call the lower Truckee an evening stream. For that matter, most of the rivers in this immediate summit area of the Sierras fish better toward the close of day, particularly if one wishes to work a dry. Generally, only small fish are taken on the surface during the day, with the larger browns and rainbows responding only to dredging. But dusk is another matter. Dusk and the low water of late spring through the fall signal the time to be on the lower Truckee.

It is difficult to classify the Truckee as to water type. In some sections there are riffles with defined pools, in others there are seemingly endless miles of pocket water; then there are areas that are boulder strewn, with enough depth to make wading perilous. Throughout most of its length, the surface is broken enough so that big, visible dries are the preferred offerings. Some of the more popular patterns are the Horner Deerhair, Muddler (greased), and variations of floating hairwing flies tied streamer-style. What all these flies share in character are floatability and a prominent silhouette.

One of my favorite patterns is a hairwing Royal Coachman tied on a
No. 10 hook. The wing is made from white calf-tail snipped near the
base where the thickness and kinkiness of the hair is such that it will
help to trap air. After this fly is heavily dressed with Mucilin, it is almost
unsinkable. This makes it perfect for riding rough, broken water, and it
is extremely visible when the only light remaining on the water is the af-
terglow from the evening sky. I believe these particular flies produce so
well because they give the impression of large caddis, which are prevalent on many big Western rivers.

Trout, particularly big browns, will move into shallower water in
the evening to feed. This schedule eliminates heroic wading and produces some fine dry-fly fishing. For this shallow-water trouting, tippets
of under 6-pound test are not needed, and repeated casting to a run will
often induce a fish to rise. Since working fish are not always visible, it's
best to seek out spots like the edge of smooth water next to a heavy
riffle, the tail of a riffle where it begins to flatten out, and secondary
flows that would not be good holding water during the day. Almost any
kind of cast from whatever is the most appropriate angle, so long as it is
drag free, can be used without fear of putting fish down.

The Trinity River, the major tributary to the Klamath in northern
California, was once a great river for steelhead. Though the dam at
Lewiston was to adversely affect the runs in the upper section, by the
time I began to fish the Trinity many steelhead were still returning. It
was here that I was baptized as a dry-fly steelheader—an unexpected
but happy event, because by the mid-1960s browns were already well
established, and I had really come for them.

Serious anglers know it is often productive to be on the water at
first light. This was my practice on the Trinity and the reason I found
some tremendous fishing. Beginning in October and continuing through
November, when the larger steelheads arrived, smaller fish—called
"half-pounders"—appeared near Lewiston. About the only time you'd
see them was in the very early morning at the tail of certain pools. With
their backs breaking the surface, they would roll, taking midges and
small mayflies. This activity would last until the sun rose and then end
abruptly.

These so-called half-pounders weighed up to 4 pounds, and I've
never hooked a faster swimmer in fresh water, except possibly fresh,
summer-run fish. Their aerobatics were sensational. And as soon as they
touched down, they'd be off again at top speed. Since the taking time
was always so brief, we never took many of them in a given morning,
but they were remarkable fish. Wise anglers purposely use a dry fly for

such fish—and with great success—in the lower reaches of the Klamath in early October.

As I learned more about the steelhead in the Trinity, I began to take a few heavy, mature fish on dries. The gala occasions on which this happened were not too frequent, but they were relatively predictable. Unlike the resident rainbows, which were riffle and pool fish, the steelhead preferred to hold in three- to eight-foot runs. After laying in a particular area for a prolonged length of time, the resting steelhead soon learned to feed, like the river rainbows, on the midday hatches. The only times fish were found at the head of a riffle were when they were on the move, and these unsettled voyagers did not respond to the dry fly.

Below Lewiston the Trinity has shallow riffles, but the pools are too deep to wade. To best fish this section you need a boat. The waters are calm here, and I prefer a canoe because of its maneuverability and quietness. Since canoes are not designed to hold well at anchor in heavy water, I usually use this type of craft chiefly for transportation, though if I see fish rising, I can rarely resist casting to them.

Almost all mature steelhead taken on dry flies by average fishermen are fish near the end of their upstream migration; the longer they hold in a particular spot, the more vulnerable they become. However, dedicated, experienced anglers do take fish in midmigration. One of the

Fong's large-river favorites: 1. Sofa Pillow Trude. 2. Buck caddis. 3. Royal Wulff. 4. Muddler Minnow. 5. Horner Deer Hair.

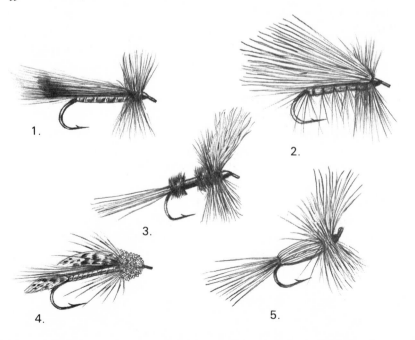

most skilled of these veterans is Frank Moore. Prior to 1974, he and his wife, Jennie, were the proprietors of the Steamboat Inn, near Steamboat Creek. For more than twenty years Frank fished the North Fork of the Umpqua in Oregon. The river, which is big water, is famous for its summer-run steelhead, and Frank is a master of dry-fly fishing for these superb game fish.

Frank suggests sighting one's fish first. This is often best done by driving the road that borders the river. Next, you should position yourself so that you can adequately cover a hold. Do not use the common technique in which a floating line is used to quarter a slightly submerged fly across a lie; instead, use a cast, which will make each drift as dragless as possible.

Normally, one would expect the evening hours, during the caddis hatch, to be the best time to present an offering. But this isn't the case. It is Frank's experience that the midday hours are the magic moments to fish a dry, and this is fortunate, because these hours also offer the best lighting conditions for sighting fish.

Two of Frank's favorite flies are a grasshopper and a caddis. These, in size 8, are usually fished on a 4-pound-test tippet, though 6 pounds can be used if the water is slightly off color. Both flies have served well: to date, Frank's largest steelhead is a bright 14-pounder. This and other trophies bring skeptics to heel when they doubt the potential of taking these magnificent fish in midmigration on the surface.

The Umpqua, like many other big Western rivers, can mean perilous wading. A wading staff can be a true friend, and cleats or sandals fitted with spikes are mandatory. The bed of this river is laced with crevices between the lava formations, and these outcroppings are the "platforms" from which casts are made. While searching for the best position, until one gains confidence, it is often more than a thrill just to shuffle from one lava ledge to another.

Long casts are necessary, and a rod of 10½ feet is not out of place. This length will allow the competent angler to use steeple casts in those situations where cliffs or foliage prevent backcasts and there are no other alternatives for reaching some of the better holds on the river. Sometimes lies are so far distant that the double haul can be extremely helpful.

On many Western rivers a boat becomes a necessity. Floating or drifting enables a fisherman to reach waters inaccessible from the road or by wading and can also be an extremely pleasurable way to fish.

Basically there are two kinds of float trips. For really big fast waters, specialized crafts patterned after double-ended dories are the most

practical. From these floating platforms an angler can cast while the boatman steadies and positions the craft. It takes years to master the handling of these drift boats, so most of them are owned by professional guides. One of the most famous groups are those men and one woman who run the lower Madison River in Montana; some of their most exciting trips are during salmon fly time, when huge trout rise to the surface in frantic attempts to gorge on the big, returning, egg-laying female flies. By using a boat they can locate and fish the most productive section of the hatch. Bookings on these or any other float trips are memory-book experiences, highlighted by casting to fish while the boat is moving and landing to fish a dry fly from suitable shallow areas on shore.

For the man who floats alone or with a partner, certain rules are mandatory, especially when a strange river is navigated for the first time. It is always important to get firsthand, reliable information about any possible difficulties or dangers downstream. If this isn't possible, before any drift is attempted an intimate survey of the proposed route, by foot or by car, is more than good practice. Once afloat, the voices of downstream riffles and drops always advise caution. Hard, fast-running rapids checked by boulders talk the loudest; if one is unfamiliar with such cataracts or hasn't been able to check them out, the roar and then the purposeful quickening of the current allows time to react, and one need not take foolish chances but line the craft through.

In all floats the greatest danger lies in trees and logs—some barely

American shad rising to caddis.

awash, some sunken—which are lying in the water in such a way that they obstruct a boat's passage. Without warning, suddenly they are there, and during such moments life preservers may be needed and equipment should be protected and lashed down. These procedures are examples of careful preparation, and when combined with anticipation of unforeseen dangers, they are the keys to successful drifting. For the novice, an overcautious attitude at the start will develop the confidence that will eventually enable him to fish waters that only a limited few ever reach.

For anglers who relish the idea of fishing a dry, recognition of basic behavior among fish is very important. The only thing that always suggests using a floater is the sighting of fish near the surface or one rising to an insect. Sometimes species not even remotely considered dry-fly fish can be had on top. The American shad, an import from the East that has established itself in many Western rivers, is just such a fish. In California the major tributaries to the Sacramento—the Feather, the Yuba, and the American—and the mother stream itself host shad during their spring spawning run. During the high waters of May and June this surge will peak. By July and August the flow will have dropped, and shad will begin rising in the evenings to take caddis flies.

In the upper stretches of the American River, below Nimbus Dam, more and more anglers are beginning to search for these rising shad. Once the fish are located, casting to them with dry flies imitating the prevalent caddis is completely conventional. Since shad average between 2 and 5 pounds, hooking six or seven in an evening can provide excellent sport. Fishing on top for this species would never have developed had it not been for the watchwords of many big-water anglers: "Look, try, and experiment."

Fishing the dry fly in big water remains one of fly fishing's greatest challenges. The fish are often larger, the surge of currents always greater. But the unexpected is the true lure of big water.

My Favorite Places to Fish	Type of Fish	Best Time	Suggested Flies Type	Size
Henrys Fork of the Snake River, Idaho	Rainbow	June–July September	1. Green Horner 2. Olive May 3. Tricorythodes spinner	6–8 16–22 18–22
Lower Hat Creek, Northern California	Rainbow Brown	Late May, early June	1. Gray Wulff 2. Light Cahill 3. Yellow Stone	6–8 14–18 12–14
Upper Trinity River, Northern California	Rainbow Brown Steelhead	October– November	1. Quill Gordon 2. Light Cahill 3. Black Ant	16–18 16–20 10–12
Upper Williamson River, Southern Oregon	Rainbow	October	1. Light Cahill 2. Adams 3. Jack Horner (yellow)	16–20 16–18 16–18
Fall River, Northern California	Rainbow	June–July	1. Jack Horner 2. Olive May (no hackle) 3. Light Mauve May (no hackle)	6–8 16–20 16–20

Steve Raymond was born in Bellingham, Washington. He graduated from the School of Journalism of the University of Washington. As a small boy he began fly fishing in British Columbia and has been an addict ever since. He is a member and past president of the Washington Fly Fishing Club and serves as vice-president of the Museum of American Fly Fishing.

He is presently the Environmental Editor of The Seattle Times, as well as being the editor of Flyfisher Magazine. He is the author of two books, The Year of the Angler and Kamloops.

13. Still Water—Ponds and Lakes
Flies, Imitations
Where to Fish and How

Steve Raymond

THE CHALLENGE OF FISHING a dry fly on still water is very different from that of dry-fly fishing in streams, but no less difficult; the pleasures and rewards are at least as great.

The dry-fly angler on moving water must always deal with the problem of drag. On still waters he must usually deal with a total absence of motion, either of the fly or the fly line. It is, therefore, frequently necessary for him to provide the motion himself, moving the fly in a manner imitative of the natural motions of still-water insects. The lack of a current to carry the fly also provides the trout a much greater opportunity to inspect the angler's imitation before deciding whether to take it, a fact that requires still-water imitations to be dressed with extra care and attention to detail. These are the two most important differences between the traditional techniques of dry-fly fishing in streams and the ever-more-popular pursuit of rising trout in lakes and ponds.

Dry-fly anglers who have served their apprenticeships on streams, as most anglers do, must first learn to recognize and deal with the habits of still-water insects when they turn their attention to lakes and ponds. The mayfly and caddis, those friendly and familiar insects that provide stream fishermen with most of their imitative opportunities, also are important to lake and pond fishermen. But the order of their importance is reversed: whereas on most streams the mayfly imitation is paramount, on still waters the caddis often is the fly most eagerly sought by surface-feeding trout. Also, both flies usually grow larger and behave somewhat differently in lakes and ponds.

179

Stream fishermen are accustomed to thinking of the chironomid as a midge; on most lakes, ponds, and reservoirs, chironomids grow to much larger sizes, so that they cannot be thought of in such infinitesimal terms. They also provide a much greater and more important share of the trout diet.

Other insects which may play roles of varying importance to still-water anglers include damselflies, dragonflies, flying ants, and even termites, though all of these usually are of much less consequence than the caddis, chironomid, and mayfly.

The stone fly, an insect of critical importance to stream fishermen, does not live in still-water environments. And such familiar streamside terrestrials as the grasshopper and jassid also are almost totally absent from the diet of trout in still waters. Their inability to remain airborne for long distances keeps them from being swept out onto the broad, open surfaces of lakes where trout might find them in numbers large enough to stimulate a sustained rise.

The serious student of still-water dry-fly fishing is well advised to study the cycle, size, and behavior of the insects on the waters he fishes and the trout's response to them.

While there are times when dry-fly fishermen will do well on any lake or pond, the rich lakes of the Northwest—from Montana to the Pacific Coast and in Alberta and British Columbia—provide the most consistent hatches and often the largest trout. Depending upon elevation and the lateness of the season, the period from late May to early July is prime dry-fly time on these waters. As soon as the winter's ice retreats, the chironomids will hatch, and while the pupal stage of these insects undoubtedly is taken more frequently than the adult, many times adults will be on the surface in sufficient numbers to trigger a rise. The chironomid hatch continues sporadically until ice returns in the late fall.

Late May and early June is mayfly time on those lakes fortunate enough to have large hatches, and the angler accustomed to using size 16 to 24 imitations on his favorite stream will often find he needs patterns as large as No. 8 on these rich Western waters.

After mid-June the caddis begins to make its appearance, increasing in numbers day by day until the hatch peaks near the end of the month or early in July. Often it is hard for the stream angler to adjust to the size of these insects; some of the large "traveling sedges" of the British Columbia lakes may exceed an inch and a half in length, and a No. 8 3X-long hook is necessary to imitate them properly.

Special care must be taken in the construction of such large imitations, both because still-water trout have ample opportunity to inspect them and because it is difficult to make such large flies float for long periods—especially when it is necessary to move them across the surface, as it often is.

Most veteran anglers come prepared to fish two imitations of the hatching caddis. One is a sparsely dressed, low-riding fly that usually is fished with a dead drift to imitate the caddis fly emerging from its pupal shuck. Ordinarily, the body of this fly is made of wool or polypropylene yarn in colors to simulate the body of the natural insects. Hackle is palmered over the forward half of the body, and there is a thin overlay of deer hair, trimmed short at both ends, to provide flotation. The second is an imitation of the adult, more heavily dressed with larger hackle, a dark deer-hair wing, and sometimes a deer-hair overlay to cover the body as well. Maximum use of deer hair is called for to provide utmost flotation, because so often it is necessary to skate these flies over the surface for long distances to simulate the movements of the traveling sedge.

Some anglers add a third pattern with a large, upright wing to imitate the tendency of hatching caddis flies to raise their wings and dry them.

For the majority of lakes the caddis is the most important insect for dry-fly fishermen. Lakes with extensive shoals of marl or pumice seem to produce the best hatches. Sometimes such lakes also offer the opportunity for the angler to spot fish cruising the shallows, to "lead" them by casting a floating imitation in their path, and then to watch every detail of the approach, the rise, and the take—surely one of the most exciting sights in all of angling.

It takes time to learn a lake well, to learn where the fish con-

Caddis imitations for lake fishing: 1. Emerging caddis pupa. 2. Resting adult caddis. 3. Fluttering adult caddis.

1.   2.   3.

gregate, where the best hatches occur and when, and where the trout rise most consistently. Careful observation will teach the angler that trout in lakes tend to cruise in similar paths, and the majority of rises will be confined to relatively small areas. Once one of those areas is found, the angler who concentrates on it will be well rewarded.

Exploring a new lake can be a stimulating and satisfying task. A pair of Polaroid sunglasses is essential, not only to protect the eyes from the merciless glare of sun from the surface, but also to penetrate the myriad moving reflections to see what lies beneath. Since the shallows are richest in life, the angler should concentrate on them, searching for weedbeds or a shallow shoreline where trout may cruise the drop-off, waiting for hatching insects to be blown over deeper water. But one should not overlook the chance of finding a shallow shoal surrounded by deep water in the middle of a lake, for these places many times provide the most exciting angling of all. The "sunken islands" in Peterhope, Roche, and other British Columbia lakes are good examples.

If the whole lake is shallow and its bottom readily visible throughout, the trout will be more cautious and wary. Even though food may be equally abundant anywhere in the lake, the fish will tend to congregate in areas that afford them the most protection. The angler should search for these places: a weedbed growing in the center of a great expanse of marl or a rocky reef jutting from a layer of pumice.

An excellent example is Hosmer Lake, Oregon's famous fishery for transplanted Atlantic salmon. Hosmer is a very shallow lake with a pumice bottom, and the fish are readily visible almost anywhere. But it also has a number of "black reefs"—areas where dark boulders lie atop the pumice—and it is over these reefs that salmon may almost always be found feeding. Instinctively, they seem to know that the dark coloration of their backs will make them more difficult to see from above when they are over these darker areas of the lake bottom.

Trout behave in much the same way, and the rule of thumb is that when food abundance is not a factor in a lake, areas affording maximum cover to the fish are likely to produce best.

The techniques of still-water dry-fly fishing depend upon the insect being imitated, the point it has reached in its life cycle, and, to some extent, upon the weather.

Hatching chironomids, for instance, tend to sit still upon the surface, waiting for their wings to dry. On cold, moist days the drying takes longer, and the observant fly fisherman will fish his imitation with a dead-drift float.

Once the chironomid's wings are dry, it tends to test them by buzz-

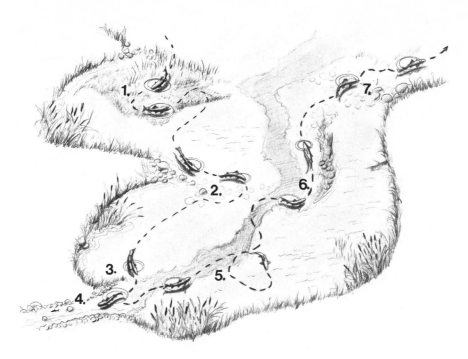

Areas on lakes or ponds where trout are most likely to surface-feed: 1. Over mossbeds. 2. Off shallow rocky or sandy points. 3. Inlet areas. 4. Mouths of feeder streams. 5. Flats along channels. 6. Around islands or humps. 7. Rocky areas offshore.

ing for some distance across the water, leaving a small wake before becoming airborne. On warm, sunny days the emerging insects will do this quickly, and the angler should skate his fly to imitate the movement. This movement also denies the trout a leisurely opportunity to inspect the imitation and see if it "looks right" before taking, which is an important factor in the strong light of a spring or summer sun.

The skating motion may be imitated by lifting the rod or retrieving the line, but the fisherman should take care to assure that he is not moving the fly too quickly or too slowly; any deviation from the normal speed of movement of the natural insect will arouse the suspicion of the trout.

Mayflies move little before leaving the surface on their maiden flights. Mayfly imitations, therefore, should be fished with no motion at all, except for whatever drift is provided by the wind. Frequently wind is much more of a problem than an ally for the still-water dry-fly fisherman. Unless he is casting directly downwind, a stiff breeze will quickly blow a belly in his line, making it impossible to set the hook in a fish that may rise to his drifting fly. It is vitally important to keep the line straight between angler and imitation at all times to ensure maximum tension on the line when the angler raises his rod in a strike. If the wind is not too strong, this tension may be kept by a very slow, gentle retrieve of the line to take up the slack caused by the riffle without moving the fly. The rod tip also should be kept low, within inches of the surface, and in a direct line with the fly; holding the rod tip high merely creates a sagging belly in the line, which makes it much more difficult to set the hook when a quickly moving trout rises to the fly.

This point cannot be overemphasized. The trout may not rank very high on the scale of intelligence, but it is very quick to recognize a fraud once it has taken it in its mouth and equally quick to get rid of it. There must be minimal slack in the line, and the angler's response to the rise must be instantaneous if he is to hook a high percentage of the fish that move to his fly; yet, it also must be a controlled response, not too vigorous, or he will lose not only the fish but probably the fly as well.

The caddis hatch offers the still-water angler the choice of a variety of techniques. The emerging caddis is best fished dead drift, because the natural insect remains stationary on the surface while struggling out of the pupal shuck. The upwing imitation, simulating a caddis drying its wings, also should be fished with a dead drift, since the natural will not move while its wings are spread. The adult may be fished either dead drift or with a rapid skating movement to imitate the travels of the cad-

Fishing slicks on a windy lake.

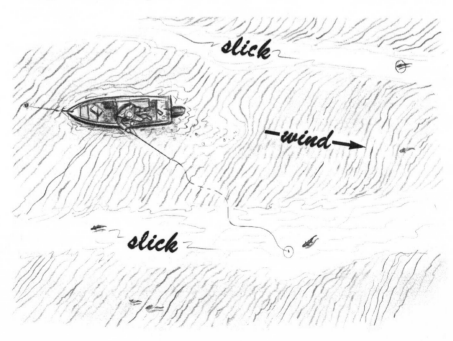

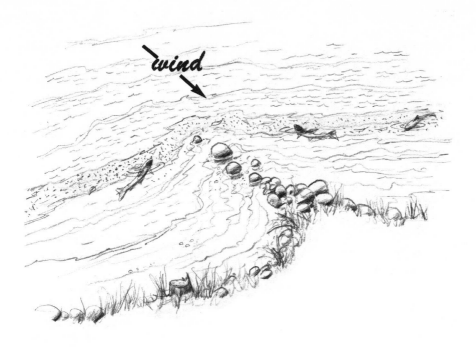

Typical "drift lines" of flotsam at a windward point.

dis. And here the angler should be especially observant to learn whether the trout are rising to stationary insects or are concentrating on those in motion and should react accordingly. Later, when the caddis return to the water for their egg-laying flights, they will be almost constantly in motion, and a skating movement by the angler is called for exclusively.

The newly emerged caddis' habit of skittering over the water before taking flight and of behaving the same way when it returns to the water for egg-laying is a special bonus for the angler on days when the wind is strong and the surface is badly broken by waves. On such days it is difficult for trout to spot a stationary insect, but they are quick to recognize a moving one by the wake it leaves behind, even in ruffled water. The quick retrieve necessary to imitate this motion is also an aid to keeping a taut line on days when the wind otherwise would blow a broad belly in any line left floating motionless on the surface.

One old and successful trick of dry-fly fishermen is to "fish the slicks" on windy days. Except when the wind is of near-hurricane proportions, there will almost always be areas on the surface—usually long, narrow stretches—that are free of riffles, and the fish have a much better chance of seeing a dry fly floating on one of these slicks than in the rough water to either side of it. When one of these slicks starts to "fill in" with riffles, another usually opens up nearby, and by following and fishing these shifting slicks, you increase your chances for success, even under marginal conditions.

Fishing the windward shore also often pays off; a strong wind will blow hatching insects toward the shore, where trout often will gather to intercept them. And sometimes, especially after a good blow, you may find "drift lines" of flotsam around points or islands, and many times these will contain spent, floating insects. If the hatch has ended for the day, trout will move into these drift lines to work them over for the survivors of earlier hatches.

Again, on cool, moist days it will take longer for the caddis to dry its wings and leave the water, thus affording the angler maximum opportunity to seduce the husky trout that lie below.

But the still-water angler does not always have to have a hatch on hand in order to successfully practice the dry-fly art. Though the main hatches subside by mid-July on most lakes, the memory of them seems to remain strong with the trout throughout the remainder of the year, and they are willing enough to rise to a floating fly in September or October. In many instances any large dry, such as a caddis or one of the Wulff patterns, fished dead drift is sufficient to stimulate a rise. But sometimes a little help is needed to trigger the desired response from the trout, and that help comes in the form of movement. A high-floating pattern skated rapidly across the surface will frequently bring many trout, even when no naturals are on the water and a dead-drift imitation produces nothing.

To employ this technique, the angler should seek out the same places that produced well for him when the spring hatches were at their height. He should fish them in the same way, but if a dead-drift imitation fails to produce, he should then start skating the fly by retrieving it as rapidly as possible. This produces a movement that is much faster than that of any natural insect on the surface, and there is no ready explanation of why it is so often effective, except to suggest that the rapid movement first gains the trout's attention and then triggers a sort of psychological response that this quickly moving thing is going to escape from him unless he attacks it instantly. A smashing strike at a fly that is being retrieved so rapidly results in many breakoffs, but it also produces many exciting moments on days when the angler might otherwise have been blanked. It seems to work even when other methods, including wet flies or nymphs, result in failure.

The tools needed to practice these techniques are not so very different from those customarily used by dry-fly fishermen on streams. The choice of a dry-fly rod is a highly personal thing, and I would not presume to recommend a particular material, action, or length, since those are decisions best left to the individual. However, it is important to note that the length of a rod is far more significant in fishing lakes and ponds than it is on small- or medium-sized streams. A long rod has a number of advantages for a still-water angler. First, it allows him to make the long casts often needed to reach fish that have risen far out, and it makes possible a longer retrieve, which is likely to be seen by more fish. Second, it is able to lift more line from the water, a critical factor when one wishes to pick up the fly quickly, turn, and cast to a fish that has just risen behind him. And perhaps most important of all, a long, stout rod is a better weapon against the strong winds that may turn an otherwise pleasant day into a nightmare succession of missed fish and wind knots.

A double-tapered floating line is adequate for many still-water situations, particularly on small ponds where many times the surface is flat calm and seldom stirred by riffles. On larger lakes or reservoirs a weight-forward floater is best for long casts into the wind, and the added size and weight of the forward belly is unlikely to frighten fish in such broad waters.

Reels for still-water fishing should have sensitive drags and plenty of capacity for backing. A large, well-conditioned trout in a lake can take out an incredible amount of line in a very short time, and you will experience a special sort of consternation when you see the last few turns of backing evaporate from your wildly spinning reel. The reel should have capacity for at least 75 yards of backing; 100 yards is not too much.

Leaders are extremely important. Because trout in still water may have the chance to inspect your fly very carefully before deciding whether to take it, they will quickly notice your leader if it is too large or too short or if it is floating. This is especially true in clear, shallow lakes where anything that casts a shadow, such as a floating leader, is an instant warning to the trout. Experience indicates that 11 feet of leader is a good minimum; 13 feet or more is better. The tippet strength must be a compromise between visibility and the size of the fish you are likely to catch. Obviously, a 7X tippet stands little chance against a highly conditioned 6-pound trout. You should test for yourself the visibility of various tippet sizes in the water and choose the strongest one that does not appear obvious. If you are satisfied that your imitation and technique are correct but still are unable to attract trout to your fly, the trouble probably is with your leader, and it is time to go to a lighter tippet, even at the risk of breaking an occasional fish.

But even the lightest, strongest leader is useless for still-water fishing if it does not sink. You can do one of two things: pray for a good riffle that will disguise your floating leader, or apply something to it that will make it sink. I have yet to find any foolproof means of sinking leaders. At the risk of naming brands, I would venture that Seidel's "600" Leader Sink is the best of the commercial products, though it is far from infallible. Various brands of toothpaste and shampoo, as well as other drugstore concoctions, have been advanced as leader sinks, and while these may make your tippet sink for a few casts, they will quickly wash off and leave it floating high and dry again. Mud and saliva work no better.

The problem of the floating leader seems to be one for which no completely adequate solution has yet been found.

It is no less vital for the fly to float than it is for the leader to sink. Keeping a dead-drift fly afloat is not much of a problem, but if you are rapidly skating the fly for long distances across the surface, it can become a serious problem indeed. Fortunately, this problem has been solved. There are a number of good dry-fly dressings available commercially, and again, at the risk of mentioning brand names, I would unhesitatingly endorse Mucilin paste and a new product known as Gehrke's Gink. A liberal dose of either of these, with occasional false casts to dry the fly, should keep any properly constructed dry fly afloat for a long period, even if it is being retrieved rapidly on every cast.

One should be careful, however, not to get any dressing on the point or barb of the hook. This may make the hook so slippery that it will slide out as easily as it goes in, resulting in lost fish. Care also should be taken not to handle leader tippets with fingers that have been used to apply dry-fly dressing, or the tippet will float no matter what you do.

Perhaps the most important tool of the still-water dry-fly fisher is the one that gets him to the fish. It may be a pair of waders, a float tube, a rubber raft, or a boat. Each has advantages and limitations.

Many lakes, reservoirs, and ponds may be fished successfully from shore by anglers wearing waders. The advantages are obvious: low cost and ease of transportation and storage. But the disadvantages are also great: if the rise is going on around a shoal a mile from shore, the angler may as well pack up and go home.

Wading a lakeshore can be a very pleasant, revealing, and rewarding experience, but the angler's effective range is so limited that one who expects to spend a lot of time fishing such waters should outfit himself with at least one other means of reaching the fish.

Float tubes have become an increasingly popular method of fishing lakes and ponds. They share with waders the advantages of low cost and easy transportation and storage. They have the important extra advantage of extending the angler's range. They also are light enough to be easily carried into mountain lakes or over trails to waters that are inaccessible by road. But there are two disadvantages to float tubes: of necessity, the angler is so close to the surface of the water that he lacks a good vantage point from which to spot rising fish or rises to his own fly. And a float tube is simply not big enough to tackle many of the large, windswept and often dangerous Western lakes.

Rubber rafts are similar to float tubes in both advantages and limitations. But a light sheet of plywood in the bottom of a rubber raft makes it a much more substantial and useful craft. It even allows the angler to stand, giving him a vantage point above the water from which to spot cruising or rising fish and to keep a constant visual check on his own fly.

Most serious anglers who fish lakes and reservoirs invest in boats of the cartop variety. Usually these are made of aluminum, fiberglass, or wood. All offer the advantages of maneuverability, a high vantage point above the water, a stable casting platform, and relative safety from all but the fiercest winds.

Aluminum boats are lightweight, virtually maintenance free, and are able to endure a lot of abuse. They have the disadvantage of being very noisy, but many anglers have solved this problem by placing rubber

Tubing, with special float tube, waders, and swim fins.

mats or layers of indoor-outdoor carpeting in the bottoms of their boats to deaden sound.

Fiberglass boats share the attributes of being maintenance free and able to withstand abuse, and they are not as noisy. But often they are heavy and difficult for one man to load on or off a vehicle.

Wooden boats may be heavy or light, depending upon their design, and usually they cost much less than fiberglass or aluminum. But they require continual maintenance and generally have a shorter lifetime.

It is significant perhaps that of all the chapters in this book, only one is devoted to dry-fly fishing in still water. It is no secret that the traditions of dry-fly fishing are deeply rooted in the art of floating a fly on moving water, and there is great mystique in the lore of the careful stalk, the cautious approach, the cast, and the final float of the fly over a feeding trout in a stream. Likewise, it is no secret that some dry-fly stream anglers have a condescending view of those who practice the art on still waters, regarding them as only a step or two above devotees of the worm or equally malodorous methods.

Yet dry-fly fishing in still water is growing rapidly, as anglers continue to discover its rewards and develop new techniques to reap them. It still lacks the rich tradition and literature of the dry fly in fast water, but these are things that will grow with the passage of time. For those

CHRISTINE FONG

who have served their apprenticeship on lakes and ponds, there is no question about the legitimacy of the method or the fact that it is equally as difficult and challenging as dry-fly fishing in streams, and perhaps in some respects more so.

And there is absolutely no questioning the rewards of still-water dry-fly fishing, as witnessed by any angler who has seen a magnificent trout thrust itself through the surface to seize the fly, then flash away in a long, sprinting run across the shoals to end with a wild, cartwheeling leap, its silver sides flashing in the sun.

The ideal is that all devotees of the dry fly should be at home on still water or fast, and that the pleasures and rewards of both methods should be mysteries to none.

My Favorite Places to Fish	Type of Fish	Best Time	Suggested Flies Type	Size
Dry Falls Lake, Central Washington	Rainbow Brown	May	1. Deerhair brown sedge	12
			2. Pink Lady (local version)	12
Hosmer Lake, Central Oregon	Salmon (landlocked Atlantic)	June	1. "Salmon Candy"	8
			2. Deerhair brown sedge	8
			3. Dark Blue Upright	16
Lundbom Lake, South Central British Columbia, Canada	Rainbow (Kamloops)	June– early July	1. Deerhair green sedge	8 3XL
			2. Deerhair brown sedge	8
			3. Slate Drake	12
Firehole River, Yellowstone National Park, Wyoming	Rainbow Brown	August	1. Joe's Hopper	8–12
			2. Hatchmatcher (numerous variations)	14–22
Hihium Lake, South Central British Columbia, Canada	Rainbow (Kamloops)	September	1. Deerhair brown sedge	8–12
			2. Deerhair gray sedge	8–12
			3. Golden Ant	12

Dave Whitlock is an illustrator, author, artist, photographer, lecturer, and instructor of fly fishing and fly tying, whose skills are totally committed to the sport and to those conservation programs that support our ecology.

He has written articles for Field & Stream, Sports Afield, *and* Outdoor Life *and is a columnist for* Fly Fisherman *magazine and associate editor of* Flyfisher. *He serves as a senior adviser of the Federation of Fly Fishermen and as adviser to the American League of Anglers.*

The thanks of all trout fishermen are due him as the inventor of the Whitlock Vibert Box, and in 1976 he was the recipient of the Max Anders Wild Trout Conservation Award.

He lives with his wife and two sons on the White River near Mountain Home, Arkansas, where he created the Whitlock Sculpin, Dave's Hopper, and other special trout, bass, and saltwater patterns.

14. Bass and Panfish Take a Fly

Attractor Flies, Hair Flies, Equipment, and Catching Fish

Dave Whitlock

FISHING DRY FLIES for bass, most species of lesser sunfish, and panfish is an extremely interesting, productive, and exciting sport. Yet only a few of the millions of catches on floating flies each year by fly fishers can be truly characterized as fish caught by the traditional dry-fly fishing to which this book is dedicated. Therefore, by defining more closely the two main methods of catching game fish by "floating" or "surface" riding flies, some of the confusion and overlap can be cleared up. Such a realization and understanding will open up many new fishing possibilities to the fly fisher for bass and panfish.

BASS BUGS, HAIR BUGS, AND SPONGE BUGS

There are a great variety of floating flies that utilize various carved or trimmed-to-shape materials for flotation. Some of these are cork, balsa wood, air-celled plastics, hollow deer hair, and sponge rubber. With shaped heads, bodies, legs, and tails, these flies float on the water surface at varying angles and levels and simulate or imitate a wide range of real and unearthly living creatures. They wiggle, crawl, twitch, dart, pop, plunk, bubble, dive, and kick according to design and animation signals given by the fly fisher down the rod-line-leader connection. Any bug in the entire animal kingdom that can fit into a bass or panfish mouth is fodder. Bass and panfish are ferociously predacious and attack almost anything that is not set on eating them! Usually bug fishing or "buggin' " is the most universal method of top-water fly fishing for the various bass species, as well as panfish such as bluegills, redear, green sunfish, crappie, white bass, shell crackers, etc. Although "buggin' " is

195

not the subject of this book, I have included this paragraph to define this method and eliminate confusion from the term "dry-fly fishing" for bass and panfish.

THE DRY FLIES

Feathers, furs, hair, and synthetic-fibered flies tied so that they float on the water's surface, and dressed exactly as those traditionally recognized as trout dry flies, will be my topic. All these flies simulate or imitate surface hatching or active adult aquatic or terrestrial insects. Fishing the dry fly for bass, particularly the spotted or Kentucky, the largemouth, and, to a lesser extent, the smallmouth, is seldom given serious consideration except by a few fly fishers. Interest quickly decreases the farther you look west and south of Pennsylvania. Panfish, especially the bluegill, has been a popular target of dry-fly fishing throughout most of the gill's prime waters. Yet in all but a few isolated circumstances, I've never found fly fishers taking the orthodox method to heart as much as it deserves.

I'm sorry to say the stigma of coarseness placed on these cool- and warm-water species carries into the tackle, flies, and methods. True, most of these plentiful species appear to be overwilling and nonselective. They also sometimes inhabit more sluggish and obstructed water than trout or salmon, but don't let me mislead you about water at this point. All three species of bass and some panfish are sometimes found in very troutlike streams, but to thrive they usually require warmer water. Ideal temperatures for these fish range from 60 to 80 degrees Fahrenheit, while trout prefer 45 to 65 degrees.

Yet even in this age of bass boats, jelly worms, fish-finders, and $100,000 bass tournaments, a beautiful and simple fact hasn't changed: the fish must eat something besides plastic worms, spinner baits, crank plugs, or pork rinds. At least one third or more of most bass and panfish diets are made up of aquatic and terrestrial insects—natural live foods.

With this knowledge and a good sensible selection of dry flies and appropriate tackle, fly fishers can find virgin fishing for bass and panfish in almost every lake, river, pond, or creek near where they live. Hatches of mayflies, stone flies, crane flies, sedges, damselflies, dragonflies, dobsonflies, and various water beetles are eagerly awaited and taken by these fish. Their nymphs and winged adults stimulate feeding that is almost as characteristically selective as found on trout streams. Spring, summer, and fall months also provide a bonus—hosts of floating, struggling, terrestrial insects such as spiders, grasshoppers, beetles, and crickets.

The Kentucky bass is on a par with the smallmouth in taking floaters and being unwilling to surrender them.

Well, then, if all this is true, why hasn't more been written and done about this hidden sport? I feel there are two groups of anglers who don't seem to want to bend their ways even a little bit to prospect this area. First, trout people usually look down their noses at bass and pan-fish. Their attitude is, "Why go for hamburger when you can have filet mignon?" Then there are the bass men. Fly fishers or bait-casters for the most part enjoy the sheer rawbone challenge of meeting a bass head on with the newest space-age lure and muscle tackle they can put together. They love the fastest, most efficient way to fill the live wells in their boats, and they often quip, "If you must play with a bass, do so after you get him in the boat!" So the idea of using the dry fly with these fish has been almost entirely neglected. This shouldn't be; it is a world of fun, a most challenging and productive method.

THE FLIES

Dry flies for bass need seldom be unique as to color and design. However, the larger sizes, 12 up through 2, will interest more good bass than the sub-12s. This applies to both match-the-hatch and attractor fishing.

Panfish such as bluegill, crappie, and the redear bream seem to closely parallel trout in their preference for naturals and attractor patterns of 10 through 18—sometimes even smaller. They will often strike large patterns, however, while not being totally serious about dining on them. This overenthusiastic trait misled me for years. Now with sizes under 12 I catch more and much larger selective panfish than with the sizes above 12!

Remembering its huge mouth and characteristic murderous surface strikes on bass bugs, I've sometimes overestimated how small a dry fly would really interest a bass. This fish can tip and sip it as delicately as any brown trout! Usually this soft rise to small floating naturals goes unnoticed or is mistaken for a chub feeding.

I once had in my aquarium a pet largemouth of about 14 inches that loved houseflies. He would take the swatter-stunned fly so softly below the surface that he wouldn't even disturb the surface with his gentle sucking in of each offering. Over the years I can recall many instances of hooking a nice bass while fishing for bluegills or green sunfish with tiny sub-10 bugs or dry flies. The last one I remember was a 7-pounds-plus largemouth that sipped in a little barbless hairwing caddis.

I prefer standard wire hooks such as the Mustad 94840, 94845, and 94831. High flotation is not usually important, nor is it necessary to use fine wire to effect hook-point penetration. Neither bass nor panfish is generally leader-shy, so the largest size of leader tippet practical per size

Black and white crappie feed heavily on day and nighttime hatching aquatic insects.

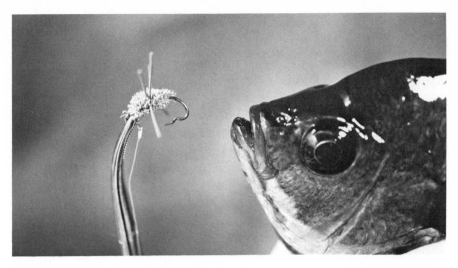

A barbless hook can be removed quickly and harmlessly from the small tender mouths of most panfish.

of fly allows efficient hook setting. Bass have an irritating habit of biting down hard on a fly and preventing point movement into the mouth walls or lips when the hook is set too lightly.

However, for most panfish and particularly for bluegill, redear, or other smallmouth sunfish, a dry fly tied on a barbless hook is a great asset. The hook point penetrates faster and holds well on the characteristically strong underwater tug-of-war used as fighting tactics by most panfish. When it comes to unhooking for release or keeping, the barbless hook comes out of the dime-sized mouth quickly, easily, and

The simplest dry flies often bring up the largest and most selective bluegill.

harmlessly, leaving the fish's tender mouthparts and your fly in almost original condition.

When bluegills are smacking up dries, it is possible to take twenty or thirty fish an hour using the barbless method. Barbless flies also intensify the excitement when you hook a good fish that you want to land.

I prefer the most durable materials for most bass and panfish dry flies: hairwings and tails, clipped deer hair or dubbed bodies, and hackles that have had their bases reinforced with fine wire or thread and thinned rod varnish. Each pattern gets a five-minute bath in liquid 3-M Scotchgard as soon as the varnish and head cement set up. I then use Mucilin for maximum flotation. Such a two-way waterproofing makes for long flotation, even with lots of fish chewing on them. I use a heavy-duty Kleenex to squeeze water out and clean fish slime off after each catch.

Here are two lists of dry-fly designs I find most useful for bass and panfish. Variation of pattern, color, and hook size is according to the particular hatch, water condition, or attraction of the fish to live suggestive or nondescript insects.

Bass
(Sizes 2 to 12)

1. Sofa Pillow, Trude
2. Wulffs
3. Muddler Minnow
4. Hairwing buck caddis
5. Elk-hair extended-body hairwing paradun
6. Elk-hair extended-body dragonflies and damselflies with spent hairwing
7. Bivisible
8. Dave's Hopper and Cricket
9. Spentwing Irresistible
10. Humpy

Panfish
(Sizes 10 to 18)

1. Spentwing Adams
2. Wulffs
3. Hairwing Irresistible
4. Comparadun
5. Polywing Spinner
6. Jassids, beetles, ants
7. Dave's Hopper
8. Bivisible
9. Spiders, skaters
10. Humpy

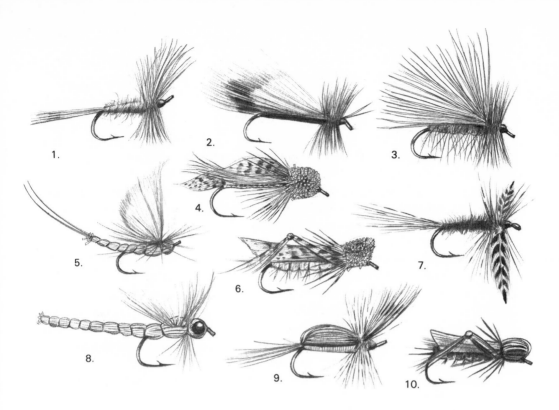

Effective patterns for all three bass: 1. Wulff Dry. 2. Trude Sofa Pillow. 3. Buck caddis. 4. Bigheaded Muddler. 5. Elk-hair paradrake. 6. Dave's Hopper. 7. Spentwing Adams. 8. Dragonfly. 9. Humpy. 10. Dave's Cricket.

Barbless flies for panfish: 1. Bivisible. 2. Comparadun. 3. Spider. 4. Irresistible. 5. Polywing Spinner. 6. Jassid. 7. Beetle. 8. Dave's Hopper. 9. Deer-hair ant.

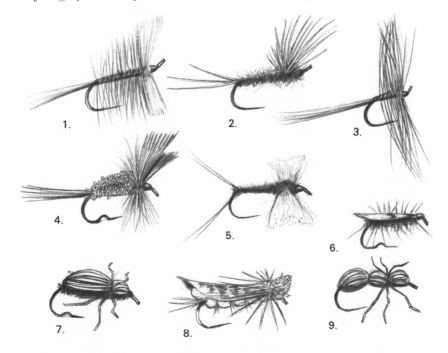

TACKLE

Rods, reels, lines, and leaders for fishing dry flies can be quite well related to trout. Panfish require less tackle refinement and put less strain on components than bass. For panfish I use tackle that spans the 3- to 5-weight ranges; for bass, from 5- to 7-weight outfits. Neither of these do much distance running but are cover-loving fish. You need a heavier leader to control your quarry in these hazardous areas, but you will seldom, if ever, see the end of a standard length fly line go out through the guides from their runs.

Rod lengths from 6½ to 8½ feet are most practical. Rod material is personal, I feel, as these days there are fine rods made of graphite, bamboo, and glass. Today and tomorrow graphite offers the best casting and fishing performance. I prefer either standard floating weight-forwards or the special bass-bug floating weight-forwards for most bass and panfish dry-fly work. With either I can also quickly switch to bugs or get a little extra distance when needed. The bass-bug taper will pull a larger dry through the air and turn it over with more authority.

A double-taper floater false casts a little easier, mends better, and roll casts easier at distances past thirty or forty feet. However, few bass and panfish dry-fly situations call for these regularly.

I use the 7½- and 9-foot knotless tapered leaders and usually add a tippet section of twenty to thirty inches with a double surgeon's knot. For bass I prefer tippets from 0-x to 3-x for patterns from size 2 down to size 10. The knotless design allows for easier fishing in the weedy or brushy waters that these fish seem generally to prefer.

For me the single-action reel is the most appropriate tool for making this kind of fishing enjoyable. Automatics can be used, but their looks, weight, mechanical operation, and performance while casting and fighting a fish does not equate with the single-action fly reels.

Smallmouth bass will regularly make rather hard runs when hooked in open and/or swift water. In this situation, giving line will prevent breakoffs. Allowing such a fish to go to the reel is impossible with an automatic, but it is a simple and exciting experience with the single-action.

Backing for the twenty-five- to thirty-yard fly line isn't regularly critical for preventing the bass from running breakoffs, but it does serve a useful purpose: It fills up the spool of the reel to a level that keeps the fly line from setting up into tight, kinky coils. Also, of course, it provides ever-present insurance should you hook a real brute that is also a track star. Twelve- or eighteen-pound-test braided Dacron backing is usually an excellent choice. Braided nylon is a very good second choice. Never use monofilament for backing!

Fishing attractor and natural-imitation dries for bass or even the less selective panfish is quite similar to the same methods effective for trout and Atlantic salmon. There is one exception: In slower water with smooth surfaces, bass still prefer some imparted action. Stream small-mouth are most troutlike, being more fast-water oriented insect feeders than either the Kentucky "spotted" or largemouth.

In any circumstance, fly presentation and its attitude on the water surface should simulate life. When fishing hatches, the fly should come floating to the holding fish or should wait on the surface for a cruising fish, but at the right moment short, erratic twitches seem to excite a bass more than just motionless or dead-drift presentations.

Fishing adult egg-laying insect imitations, as well as big terrestrials such as crickets, spiders, and grasshoppers, is another method. Bass respond well to visual on-the-spot presentations. Any insect fluttering down and splashing on the surface is seldom refused by any bass that sees it land. In fact, they will often come out and meet it halfway before it hits the water! Larger spent or bucktail hairwing patterns especially, that come down slower and on the surface, enable the fly fisher to twitch or skate them like live insects. The Spentwing Irresistible, Buck-tail Caddis, Sofa Pillow, and bivisibles are excellent patterns for this type of fishing.

No matter what method or type of pattern I use, I generally read

Stream smallmouth are most troutlike, being moving-water aquatic insect feeders.

the water intensely to locate good cover or holding areas. During spawning time, bass and panfish nesting areas are prime spots to work dries over. Moss beds, pockets, lilies, cattails, reeds, overhanging tree limbs, fallen trees, logs, brush, boulders, stumps, rock ledges, and cut-banks are a few cover areas that most bass and panfish hide in to ambush their prey. Spot-target casting to these cover-holding areas provides an extra source of enjoyment as well as an intense sense of expectancy.

Fishing most of the smaller, clear, fast and slow, mountain bass streams requires careful approaches, delicate casting, and the lighter, longer line-leader methods commonly used for selective trout. The smallmouth is an especially wary bass, but the spotted and largemouth can also be put down by a poor presentation.

Of course, on the larger rivers these fish become much easier to approach. They sense that they are more concealed by greater water depth and less clarity. A dry fly will naturally be less alarming and ini-tially more attractive to bass and panfish than the larger, heavier bass bugs and spinning and casting lures that they are pounded with every season. As I said earlier, the dry fly will expose most of us to virginlike fishing for these fish in many areas, even hard-fished ones.

For flowing waters I usually make my presentation by using a quar-tering upstream or quartering downstream cast. The upstream quarter allows a good long drift and hides you from the fish. However, it is dif-ficult to impart action to the fly or float it down into eddies or under

Often a slowed entry of a dry fly will be met halfway by an eager bass.

Bass and panfish respond equally well to most hatches that occur throughout the milder seasons.

Because bass and panfish are cover-loving ambush feeders, working such areas with a hopper or some other large dry fly is an exciting sport. A dry fly that flutters down slowly is often met before it hits the surface by an eager bass or panfish.

overhanging cover such as willow limbs. The downstream "dead" or active "life" drift presentation does not line the fish first. Using the current or wind, I can also mend the floating fly under and alongside many more fish-holding covers.

By using a downstream quartering, you can keep excessive slack out of the line and have the current's assistance to help set the hook when the take occurs. Then you are also in a splendid position to work the fish away from its cover and avoid sure tangling and breakoffs. Give the average hooked bass a few feet of slack line, such as is common with the upstream quarter, and he will run immediately to his hideout or leap and shake out the stinging hook. Bass and panfish exist in every state except Alaska and inhabit the majority of freshwater streams, rivers, ponds, and lakes. Even prime trout rivers often provide outstanding smallmouth fishing on their lower, warmer reaches. During my travels about this land, I'm regularly told by my fishing hosts that this or that water is loaded with big bass and that the trout just aren't there anymore. I quietly drool as we head another fifty miles upstream or to another watershed to cast for trout.

Bass and panfish usually respond to floating flies in streams in the same manner as trout, except that most of them prefer more fly action.

Fortunately, bass and panfish are generally on the increase. Our ever-persistent manipulation of flowing water systems either warms, slows, dams, or pollutes them. In most of these places bass and panfish seem to adjust rapidly and maintain excellent populations. Unfortunately, to date, anglers with their fly rods have not taken advantage of this fundamental fact.

Dry flying just as you would for trout can provide you truly limitless hours of excellent, enjoyable angling. An orange-breasted, saucer-sized bluegill or thickly muscled, crimson-eyed smallmouth will take the dry fly most willingly and is usually far more reluctant to give it up than a lot of trout we fish for today!

My Favorite Places to Fish	Type of Fish	Best Time	Suggested Flies Type	Size
Quetico Provincial Park lakes and rivers, Ontario, Canada	Smallmouth	July–August	1. Hexigenia Brown Drake Elkhair Spinner	6–12
			2. Dave's Cricket	4–8
			3. Muddler Minnow	2–8
Area between Alligator Alley and Everglades	Largemouth	February– June	1. Bivisible Sofa Pillow	2–10
			2. Trude	2–10
Tailwaters of Grand River System in Oklahoma: Pensacola Dam, Hudson Dam, Ft. Gibson Dam	Largemouth	May–June	1. Muddler Minnow	4–12
			2. Hairwing Buck Caddis	
			3. Dave's Hopper	
Big Hole River, between Melrose and Wise River, Montana	Brown Brook Rainbow Grayling	August– mid-October	1. Dave's Hopper	8–12
			2. Irresistible	10–16
			3. Muddler Minnow	6–10
White and Norfork rivers, Arkansas	Rainbow	May– November	1. Brown Caddis	16–22
			2. No-hackle Sidewinder Dun, slate olive or gray/yellow	18–22
			3. Midge Pupa	18–24

As a fisherman, Lee Wulff originated light-tackle fishing for both salt-water and freshwater fishing. He was the first angler to use animal hair for dry flies (Gray Wulff, White Wulff, etc.) and was a pioneer in sponsoring the release of game fish by anglers.

His fame is assured as a conservationist. He has been a member and chairman of the New Hampshire Fish and Game Commission and conservation adviser to the Province of Newfoundland. He is one of the founders of the Federation of Fly Fishermen and presently serves as director of the Outdoor Writers of America, the American League of Anglers, and the Connecticut River Watershed. He works hard as vice-president of the International Atlantic Salmon Association and the Atlantic Salmon Association.

He is the recipient of seven "Teddy" awards for the excellence of his film productions. A few of his clients are CBS Sports Spectacular, ABC's The American Sportsman, Warner Brothers, Universal, and Twentieth Century-Fox, as well as many major corporations.

As an author, he has appeared in the finest periodicals and currently is a contributing editor of Sports Afield. Six books have been written by this great sportsman, among which are A Handbook of Freshwater Fishing, Fishing with Lee Wulff, and The Atlantic Salmon.

15. The Dry Fly for Atlantic Salmon

Beginnings, the Best Times, and Presentations

Lee Wulff

THE ORIGIN of the dry fly for Atlantic salmon may be a little obscure. A new wet fly, fresh from the box and dry, may have floated on the surface for the first cast or two. That type of a low-floating fly is an excellent dry for salmon, and the probability is that Atlantic salmon were caught in that manner long ago.

According to an article in the British *Fisherman's Log* of 1929, serious dry-fly fishing started in 1906 with J. R. Fraser's taking salmon on the Test while fishing with floating mayfly imitations. However, World War I may well have ended Fraser's efforts. A little later, about 1914, Colonel Monell, George La Branche, and Ed Hewitt fished for salmon with the dry fly on Canadian rivers.

It was the beginning of the era of the dry fly for trout fishing in America, and it was natural that these fishermen should give dry flies a thorough tryout for salmon. Success was immediate for them. Ed Hewitt's bivisible was the most popular fly—a high-floater, quite visible to both angler and fish. However, Atlantic salmon fishing was heavy with ritual and quite patterned to the subsurface fishing; dry-fly fishing spread very slowly.

In contrast, dry-fly fishing seemed to die out in Britain. A few fishermen did catch fish on dry flies, but the general belief was that European salmon would not take a dry fly. This view still prevails, and it is true that in Britain, Norway, and Iceland, salmon are reluctant to take dry flies. During my fishing bout with "Jock Scott" on the Dee in Scotland in 1962, I took a 10-pound salmon on a size 8 White Wulff, which came as a shock to the onlookers. The late Gerry Curtis, while fishing on the Dee and other rivers, has taken fish occasionally on dry flies, as have anglers in both Norway and Iceland. European anglers, as a whole, have no faith in the dry fly.

While fishing in Iceland I ran a comparison test between dry and wet flies. Choosing a well-rested pool on a warm and pleasant day (on two different rivers, the Grimsa and the Hafjardera), I went through the pool three times with a dry fly—once each with a White Wulff, a surface stone fly, and a skater. Then I followed the dry-fly fishing by going through the same water three times with wet flies. The results were the same in each case: No rises at all to the dry fly and three fish hooked during the wet-fly fishing in each river. All of which proved to me that while dry flies may take fish on European rivers, the method is not anywhere nearly as productive as the subsurface fly.

In Iceland there are few hatching insects in the rivers, which may explain the lack of interest in dry flies by the salmon there. In Norway there is a circumstance that mitigates against dry-fly fishing. Norwegian rivers are relatively cool; most of them are fed by snow from the mountains throughout the summer. Therefore, on a hot day the snow melts faster, but the river water temperature, due to the freshly melted snow, drops. The colder water on warm days may inhibit the dry-fly rise. On almost all the European rivers there are plenty of aquatic insects, and beyond that I do not know why European salmon are so reluctant to rise to a dry.

Salmon fishing with wet flies is almost as old as half a millennium. Serious dry-fly fishing is about half a century old and limited to Canadian rivers; naturally, it is still developing. A new combination of colors and shapes for underwater fishing is hard to come by after the centuries during which the Atlantic salmon anglers of the world have been inventing and testing their ideas. With dry flies there are still new categories to be discovered and color combinations to be tried in each one. This lends a special interest for those salmon anglers who tie their own flies or who are involved with flytiers who are having new ideas which can be tested.

The relative effectiveness of the dry fly to the wet depends upon three things. The first is the water temperature and the stream conditions. When the water is cold the fish do not rise well. The key to when the water is warm enough for dry flies, which may vary in temperature from stream to stream, is usually given by the salmon themselves. When they begin to show themselves by rolling to the surface or "porpoising," they are ready. The warmer the water, the better the chances of the dry-fly angler versus the wet-fly fisherman.

The second important factor is the coverage of the fly. The free-floating dry fly drifts directly downstream. Its coverage per cast is very small in comparison with the wet fly, with which an angler can sweep a pool from side to side for its full length. The dry-fly angler needs a more precise knowledge of where the fish are to make up for his limited water coverage per cast. This is restricted not just by the free drift, but also because the limited time before the current causes drag on the fly further shortens the time that the fly is properly fishing the water on each cast.

The third factor, which favors the dry-fly fisherman, is that the low, warmer water of summer tends to concentrate the salmon in groups in the pools. These resting places or concentration points are usually well known or easy to recognize, and the angler can focus his fly coverage right where the fish are. Every Atlantic salmon angler should realize that it is not just water coverage but concentrated fishing over the precise spots where the fish lie that brings success.

Although the overwhelming share of his time will be spent with a free-drifting fly, a dry-fly fisherman may use fly motion on occasion. The skater is an excellent fly to tease salmon with. The more erratic the teasing motion, the more chance there is of drawing a rise from a jaded salmon. But the more erratic the motion, the more likely the salmon is to miss the fly. Skaters, by their very nature, must be on small hooks, which also makes hooking a fish more difficult. (To fish the skater well, the leader and line should be greased and floating.)

A second dry-fly motion that is effective is a small twitch or jerk of the fly just as it reaches or passes over the fish. This is a sort of do-or-die effort, which I save until the last cast I plan to make over a given fish or known salmon lie. I believe this little twitch is likely to put a fish down completely if it does not elicit a rise.

Presentation and choice of fly are, of course, the key to success with the dry fly. Should the dry fly drop right over a fish's nose and then drift over him? Should it approach him with a drift of five feet? Ten feet? Thirty feet?

Anglers should recognize that salmon are as different from one another as people are. One fish may succumb to a long float, another to a fly that dropped on his nose. The wise angler will use all types of float but will concentrate on the length of float that he finds most successful.

When an angler is unsure of the exact positions of the fish, he will, quite naturally, drift his dry fly over all the good water. Still, the important thing is to envision the fish below the surface, to think of particular fish in particular spots; the more accurate the angler's imaginings, the more salmon he will catch.

What flies should a dry-fly man carry, and when should he use each

White Wulff.

one? He should have high-floaters and low-floaters in several shapes and sizes. He should have sparse flies and fluffy ones, spiders and skaters.

My own technique is to have a good variety of categories of flies, giving special emphasis to changing the size and shape rather than the color.

The determination of color is a personal thing with both the angler and the fish. On one trip, when I was having fair success with my Wulff patterns—the White and the Gray (which have a natural mayfly shape and color)—I was surprised to find a companion doing just as well with the Wulff pattern made up entirely of brilliant yellow—a fly I would have instinctively avoided using.

Good salmon fishermen develop a sense of the salmon's preferences, and they must follow them to gain anything from their experience. However, if they become too hidebound to try new things or to allow for far-out thinking on the part of the salmon, they'll miss out on some good fish. It's worth checking with other anglers on the particular waters you fish to find what patterns and sizes are working at that time. A fly that wows them one year may be a dud the next. A few standards, however, seem to work reasonably well year after year.

For general fish the Wulff patterns and the bivisibles are standard; they're tried and true. The Royal Wulff has the advantage of being very visible to both angler and fish no matter what the weather and water conditions are. I tend to use it in the midrange size of 8. As I go to smaller sizes I lean toward the less flashy Gray Wulff. As I increase the size, to 6s and 4s or larger, I use the white pattern. (I've used the White Wulff successfully up to size 3/0.)

Small variations often have major effects. Sometimes I change my

Wulff pattern to include a palmer-tied hackle down the body to make it scraggly. This is a fluffier, high-floating fly, and a salmon that has refused a regular pattern will often take it.

The Rat-faced McDougal is a good basic type. The shape of the body can be changed and varied to give a broader scope. The "cigar butt," now in vogue, is essentially a McDougal variation.

I recently used a looped-hackle dry fly with success. The tail of the hackle stems are tied in at the bend of the hook and the head of the hackle stems at the head of the fly, with the hackles fanning out on each side to create a heart-shaped wing pattern like a moth. It floats with these wings flat on the surface, and when moved they have an excellent, lifelike resiliency.

Spiders and skaters have their place too. My favorite is the Prefontaine, a size 16 skater with a reverse tail or "snoot" of bucktail which projects forward from the hook and gives the skater a very erratic action.

This may be a good place to bring out the fact that although in the warm waters of summer only the smaller wet flies bring success, there seems to be no limit on the size of dry flies that will work.

Continuing with fly types and patterns, I find that the typical gray (Plymouth Rock) and brown bivisibles work well with badger, furnace, ginger, and others playing a minor role.

Adding to the categories, I like a surface stone fly which floats low on the water. It has a long, plastic body with bucktail lying down over its back. The fly floats on the bucktail, with the body in or below the surface film. It is hard for an angler to see, but the salmon has no such difficulty.

A small, dark, fat-bodied dry fly in sizes 10 and 12 has been very valuable. I make one up in all black, a Midnight, which I like to use following a big White Wulff when I have a salmon interested. It is the locating of interested salmon and working over them that brings the dry-fly angler his greatest joy. If you can find a fish that shows interest but will just look at or play with the fly rather than taking it, you've uncovered a frustrating fishing problem.

I recall one such fish, a 19-pounder, on the River of Ponds, who gave me three hours of excruciating pleasure. The water was low and clear. I saw him come up in his first rise to the size 8 Gray Wulff I was using as a search fly. He poked his nose up under the fly and made it bounce on the surface, but his mouth was tightly closed throughout the movement.

I tried two more drifts with the same fly with no action, then paused to change to a size 6 White. Fifteen casts brought no action, and

I was about to change again when the salmon rose up under the fly, held a position just under the surface while the fly floated over him, and drowned it with a splash of his tail as he went down to take up his lie again.

I changed to a surface stone fly of brown bucktail and yellow body. On the first cast he came up and broke the surface in a typical head and tail rise. But, watching the fly, I saw that he was just beyond it. It drifted by, inches from his head on my side of the fish. I've learned through long experience and training not to strike with a dry fly unless I actually see the fly go out of sight. If I had struck and yanked the fly away from its position alongside his left eye, I might well have put him down for good.

I worked over that fish for another two and a half hours and drew sixteen more rises, none of which were open-mouthed efforts to take the fly. He made a big swirling splash when he moved across behind the skater. He simply looked closely at all the others. Periodically I went back to the size 8 Gray Wulff. (I make it a rule never to leave a fish without trying again the fly it rose to first.) It was that fly, on the twentieth rise, that he finally took and was hooked and captured on.

Whereas salmon will normally hook themselves with a wet fly, the dry-fly angler must be prepared to strike and set the hook. The wet fly is fished under tension. It is moving through the water when the salmon takes it. That continuous motion pulls the hook and sets it. The dry fly drifts free without tension, and the salmon, feeling the steel and recognizing the fraud, can spit it out before the line comes tight.

Because of a salmon's proclivity for missing or rising falsely to a dry fly, many anglers become confused. They see the rise, and because they are not concentrating their attention on the fly they fail to note the false-

Lee Wulff playing a salmon on the Serpentine River, Newfoundland.

LEE WULFF

Twenty-six-pound salmon, hand-tailed and played on a light 6-foot rod and size 16 dry fly.

ness of the rise and they strike. They miss and decide that they have either struck too soon or too late. They try striking later or earlier. Then, on a true rise, they either yank the fly away before the salmon's mouth can close, or they strike after the fish has spit it out. The most common fault is to strike too soon. Most salmon are deliberate. The time to strike is when the fish starts the move back to its lie. The perfect strike comes the instant the fish's mouth has closed on the fly.

The strike should be just hard enough to set the hook. Setting the hook requires a hook movement of only about ⅛ of an inch. It is a quick pull of the line, rather than a sweeping lift of the rod, that works most effectively.

A dry-fly fisherman should have a fair coverage of fly sizes from 10s to 4s. If he's a trout fisherman too, he should take some of his favorite trout flies to use in low water conditions.

The greatest challenge in angling may be the taking of big Atlantic salmon on small trout flies. I've caught a dozen salmon of over 20 pounds on a size 16 fly in as many years, and one day I hope to take a 30-pounder on a size 16 for what may well be the ultimate angling experience.

Leaders, as the saying goes, should be just long enough and just fine enough to fool the fish. In bright, clear, low water, I may go up to twenty feet or more in length and down to three pounds in tippet test. For normal fishing twelve feet at eight pounds test is good. Shorter and heavier leaders have their place, occasionally, when the water is high and, perhaps, discolored.

Fly lines should be of the floating or slowly sinking type. I rarely grease mine, and I want the line and leader to sink but to stay near the surface for easy pickup. I grease my leader and the front of the line to fish skaters, but otherwise I prefer line and leader below the surface where they're least conspicuous.

One of the worst mistakes a dry-fly angler can make is to pick up a bad cast that lands just above the fish. If it's in his vision and the fly and line splash down and are immediately pulled away, it will disturb the fish. The rule is to let a bad cast lie until it has passed beyond the water you're fishing. Strangely enough, what an angler considers a bad cast may look good to a salmon. I've seen them come up to take a dry that was floating in the middle of a confused mess of line and leader.

As this is being written, I've just returned from a few days on the Upsalquitch. The water was low and warm, the salmon difficult. This is the kind of fishing to challenge one's skill. The fish are concentrated and have been fished over hard. They've seen every fly and combination the anglers can think of to put over them for days and days.

A Newfoundland salmon, tired and ready for the release.

LEE WULFF

My wife, Joan, and I took our two-fish limit the final evening. We'd had a lot of false rises, as the other anglers had had in the hours and days beforehand, but we found four salmon that meant business when they rose and that took our flies. Which flies? The spread may surprise you. Three took a big size 4 Gray Wulff, to our guide's astonishment, and one a size 16 Lady Joan. One was much smaller than the flies the other anglers had been using, and one was much, much larger than anything they'd seen before.

The dry fly is effective for the salmon of this continent. Many of us fish the dry fly in preference to the wet, when we feel they're equally effective, for the pure joy of seeing the fish come to the surface and show itself. Unlike the wet fly, the free-drifting dry may be put to a fish from any angle—upstream, across, or down. In a good pool an angler may find three interested fish and work one while resting the other two, all from the same position. The rises one remembers and dreams about are those that come to a dry fly.

My Favorite Places to Fish	Type of Fish	Best Time	Suggested Flies Type	Size
St. Jean River, Gaspé, Quebec, Canada	Atlantic salmon	Early July	1. Surface Stone Fly 2. Gray Wulff 3. Prefontaine	4 8 16
Restigouche River, Quebec-New Brunswick Border, Canada	Atlantic salmon	Early July	1. White Wulff 2. Surface Stone Fly 3. Looped Hackle Bug	6 2 6
Portland Creek, Newfoundland, Canada	Atlantic salmon	Early July	1. White Wulff 2. Midnight 3. Rat-faced McDougal	6 12 6
Henrys Fork of the Snake River, Idaho	Brown Rainbow Cutthroat	September	1. Pale Waterly Dun 2. Jassid 3. Adams	18 20 16
N.W. Minipi River, Labrador, Canada	Eastern brook	Early July	1. Royal Wulff 2. Black Gnat 3. Rat-faced McDougal	6 10 6

Robert Warner was born in Brookline, Massachusetts. He started fly fishing at the age of eight and has been at it ever since, including ten seasons spent on the Battenkill.

Besides the United States, he has fished in Canada, Mexico, Costa Rica, El Salvador, British Honduras, Argentina, Paraguay, Chile, Brazil, Japan, the Fiji Islands, New Zealand, Australia, India, Sri Lanka, Iran, Lebanon, Kenya, Belgium, Jamaica, Ireland, Scotland, and Norway.

His articles have appeared in many periodicals including Outdoor Life, Field & Stream, Sports Afield, Esquire, *and* True. *He is the author of* Don't Blame the Fish.

16. Peripatetic Anglers
Fishing in Norway, Quebec, New Zealand, and Argentina— A Few Tips

Robert Warner

NORWEGIANS CLAIM, and I assume correctly, that the Laerdal River has been host to more royalty than any place in the world except Buckingham Palace. Be that as it may, it is one of the world's finest Atlantic salmon and sea trout streams. I was once a guest there and killed a number of salmon of 18 to 26 pounds. They were taken on a 14-foot greenheart rod that must have weighed four pounds. It had been supplied by my host, Thomas Falk. I could hardly lift the thing.

On my last day he gave me several skater flies and suggested that I try these dries for sea trout. He said, "There's a run of trout in the river. Sea trout will rise in the heat of the day and the salmon generally won't. If you want, you can fish with that little trout rod you brought along."

The "little trout rod" he referred to was a 9-foot-6-ounce Orvis salmon rod, which he had glanced at when I first set it up and said, "A fine rod for a wee lassie. Why didn't you bring the lassie to go with it?" Then he had snorted at my salmon flies, tied on size 6 and size 8 hooks, and loaned me some flies big enough to have landed the shark in *Jaws*. I had quickly accepted the proffered greenheart rod; I didn't want one of those Norwegian boathooks impaling me in the back of the neck. Now, finally, on the last day of my visit, I would have a chance to fish dry with proper American tackle.

My gillie was a man of close to no words. I followed him downstream to a wide, deep pool. He sat on the bank, and I assumed this was the place where I was to go after the sea trout. And the trout were there, as thick as if I'd been fishing a hatchery pond. But, for reasons that were beyond me, I couldn't hook them. Over a period of an hour, or until they stopped rising, I must have missed at least twenty fish, and they were of good size, from 4 to 8 pounds.

I missed another one and swore. I glanced at the gillie sitting a few

In Norway, glaciers are the source of many salmon rivers.

feet behind me. He was placidly chewing a stem of hay. Finally the rise ended and he stood up, which meant that the fishing was over.

I turned to him and said, "I'll be damned if I can understand it. I've been a dry-fly fisherman for over thirty years, and I've never had any trouble till now. Those trout are too fast for me."

He removed the strand of well-munched hay from his mouth and said, "Trout are not too fast. You're too fast. When a fish takes the fly, you say, 'One dead Nazi, two dead Nazis, three dead Nazis,' then you strike."

All this after watching me miss twenty fish! I looked at him. He munched his hay. I said nothing and did nothing, but I was tempted to wrap two hundred dollars' worth of tonkin rod around his neck. That was many years ago; it was the last time I had a chance to use the dry fly on rising sea trout.

I will grant that I am prejudiced and often use dries when nymphs, streamers, and wets would do better. But dries have produced for me when my companions, who were using everything else, have gone fishless. Those are the days I remember.

In 1965 my wife, Sylvia, and I first fished the Papaskwasati in northern Quebec, a river that flows into the huge Lake Mistassini. We were fishing maribous and streamers, and we had caught and returned a few 4-to-6 pound brookies when the fish just quit. Sylvia said, "I told you you ought to have brought along a solunar table. Then we'd know when to start again."

I turned to our Indian guide and suggested we have lunch. He nodded and snapped his cigarette butt in a long arc to the pool's center. And up came a trout to give it a look. I said, "To hell with lunch. Let's fish dry."

In the next hour we netted seven brookies, not one under 4

This beautiful symmetrical 15¾-pound salmon was killed in Norway.

pounds. Why? There were no insects on the water, but for some reason the trout came up when they wouldn't touch anything below the surface. I have had the same experience many times with bass. You could fish wet flies, spoons, plugs, and other deep-water and diving lures without so much as a look, then put on a big dry or a tiny surface popper, give it an occasional light twitch, and take bass until your arm ached. One of the beautiful things about fishing is not the rules; it's the exceptions. And this is particularly true of the dry fly.

Until the big Quebec brookies all but disappeared, the law permitted you to take twenty-five fish a day, and it was no great trick on the Papaskwasati to wind up with 100 pounds of trout, if you were that kind of meat hunter. Happily, today you are allowed fifteen trout in possession and of those fifteen only eight a foot long or over. Of the eight you can keep just two that are 22 inches or over. Since there are no small trout, that means that you are limited to two a day. So you keep one to eat and don't kill the other unless it is big enough for the taxidermist. At long last Quebec is trying to protect what they have left and to bring back some of their almost ruined streams.

Now, how to get to Quebec's best fishing, to whom do you write, and for what time of year? You should apply at least a full year ahead, because the last week in the season, or the first week in September, is the best. Ask for the Papaskwasati; this is a longer stream with far more pools in it than the other rivers. Here the big hairwings should do well in both moving water and still. Fish the still, or almost still, pools slightly upstream, and let your fly float down below you. Then, when it starts to drag, pick it up and cast again. In the moving water cast directly upstream, and let your fly come down to you. When it is almost on top of you, pick it up and cast again a yard to one side or the other. Keep working it until you have fished all your water.

To make a reservation on the Papaskwasati or other Quebec waters, write to the Department of Tourism, Hunting and Fishing, P.O. Box 8888, Quebec City, P.Q., Canada, and ask for the first until the seventh of September. Be sure to ask about costs.

I can also suggest the Le Grande River, which was opened for the first time in 1975 and now offers virgin fishing. Literally virgin, because this is one of the largest rivers in the province and until a few years ago no one had fished it. In 1975 a chap nicknamed Figaro opened a camp on it, and, the last I heard, the guides were still taking the customers to hitherto unfished waters for 7- to 8-pound brookies and for larger lakers and northern pike. I was there in 1975 and can assure you it is hard to beat.

Take both warm and cold weather clothing. You may start out fishing in your shirtsleeves in the 80s, and at night the temperature will drop down into the 40s, with a cold rain to usher in the drop. Take waders and a wading staff. I add this because two men who were with me didn't, and they had to do all their fishing from a canoe because their hip boots were next to useless. Take big dries and the more colorful streamers.

A question I am frequently asked at the end of a talk on round-the-world fishing is, "Of all the countries where you have been, which one had the best fishing?"

The answer: "It's a tie between two countries with half a world between them, New Zealand and Argentina. And they are very different. For the dry-fly purist, New Zealand comes first, as it offers the same type of dry-fly fishing we enjoy here at home, except that the trout are much larger and far more numerous.

I have fished North Island and South Island, both rivers and lakes. Here your own skill, and not luck, is by long odds the major factor. Descendants of English and Scotch ancestors do two things a little better than anyone else: raise sheep and fly fish. If you have the good fortune to go there, I would suggest that you head for Invercargill at the bottom of South Island. This is easily wadable river fishing.

My guide there was a sheep rancher, and in the off-seasons he spent a great deal of time on the streams within twenty miles of Invercargill. His name was Tony Blake, a beautiful fisherman and as fine company as I have ever met. For a week we fished every day together. He always insisted that I take his favorite pools, and he showed me exactly how to fish them. It was close to the ultimate in dry-fly fishing, and we never came home without trout.

The world boasts a great many beautiful lakes, but my number one choice is Wanaka, also on South Island, which has a three-a-day trout limit. Our young guide, Noel Wilson, had a high-speed boat moored a few rods from our motel. Each morning Sylvia, Noel, and I raced miles up the lake to one of the shallow bays or to where a river poured down into the lake. One morning we went to the far end of Wanaka, where the mist hung close to the water and gradually rose to reveal the towering volcanic mountains plunging into the depths. It was almost too beautiful to be real.

We hauled the boat up on a gravel shore, waded out, and started casting to occasional rising trout. Then Noel came back and told Sylvia to keep on fishing where she was but for me to follow him. He had spotted four rainbows and a big brown lying in a row just a few feet apart. He told Sylvia that she couldn't cast far enough to reach them.

We went down the shore until he stopped and pointed. "See them? The brown is second from the left, about a yard from the first rainbow."

For the life of me I couldn't see so much as a sign of those fish. I said, "I want the brown, I'll try for him."

Noel nodded, then looked through my box of dry flies and picked a small dark one. "Try this. Now, move up the shore four or five feet and cast straight out. No. That was about six feet to the right. There! That's it."

The fish rose and I struck. The brown was a big one—6 pounds. I went back and tried again and took a 3-pound rainbow and released it. Noel said that was the end of it; the others had gone to deep water.

By noon, when we lunched, the mist was gone, and the steel-gray lake lay as flat as a mirror and reflected the trees along the shores and the mountains behind them. We heard only the occasional raucous squawk of a gull or the splash of a rising trout. After lunch Sylvia caught two rainbows and released them, and I caught a small freshwater salmon and did the same. We had cold beers on the shore before we started back. Sylvia said, "This is a place every fisherman in the world should see."

"Yes," I added, "and fish too."

In New Zealand go to Invercargill and ask directions of the A. W. Hamilton Company. Ask for Allen White, the manager, or for one of his clerks if he's not in. Get your dry flies here. They are a bit different from those at home, but don't try to get by with home-tied flies. Everyone in New Zealand apparently fishes the dry fly, and Mr. White and his clerks are among them. You will be appalled at the number of flies you will set aside, but wait till you hear the price—about a quarter of what you would pay at home. And while you are there, arrange for your guide. Mine came with a car and an encyclopedic knowledge of every river within twenty miles of Invercargill; there are more rivers and streams than you would care to count. Your guide will say, "Hm!" Then he will stop to figure the weather, the rise or fall of a particular stream, and announce where you are going to fish. Suffice it to say that my guide was always right, because we must have fished a dozen rivers in a week and everyone of them produced.

And if you can cast at least seventy-five feet of line time after time, there is another place you should try—the Tongariro River on North Island, about a three-hour bus trip from Auckland. Fish with Tony Jensen, fishing author and master guide, in Turangi, North Island. He is a delightful person. If he is tied up with another customer, fish with his wife, who, unless you are a past master at the sport, will do a lot better than you, although she will always give you the best pools on the river.

And remember that New Zealand is below the equator, so their summer is our winter. Start your fishing trip in January and end it in April.

Argentina may still be the best, in spite of my brief experience there with dry flies. But let's start with the landlocked salmon, the exception to the rule, because it takes the dry fly just as it does in the U.S. and Canada—as if its life depended on it. I was once fishing near Esquel, far to the south of Bariloche, with one of the many Nazis who found it unhealthy to return to Germany after the war. He always approached all fishing problems with the statement, "Here it is much better to spin," and he would let fly with his hardware right into the middle of the pool I was supposed to fly fish. Then he took me salmon fishing. After a four-mile walk through herds of bulls that had me always sticking close to the fences, we finally reached an enormous pool, or what the Argentinians call a boca, where a lake flowed out to start a river. "Here it is best to spin," said my guide, hurling a large hunk of hardware into the pool's middle. "Get that *@#*#%*# spoon out of there before you put every fish in the pool down," I shouted.

He glared at me and complied. I tied on a streamer, then watched a big moth with at least a four-inch wingspread flutter into the water. The surface broke, and a huge landlock came into the air and grabbed the moth.

I took off the streamer, tied on a hairwing Coachman, and cast to the same spot. Some minutes later my guide netted the 10-pound fish, the largest landlock I have ever taken.

But this is primarily a tale of trout fishing, so a bit on how the Argentinians fish the dry fly is not to be overlooked. They fish big flies with a drag, something we carefully avoid at home. In Argentina, apparently, the more drag the better. What the fish thinks it is rising to I don't know, but it certainly is not a fly. The Argentine trout's diet consists mostly of a small crayfish called the panchora crab.

There is excellent fishing and very comfortable living at the beautiful big inn in Correntoso, roughly a fifty-mile bus trip from Bariloche and on the other side of Lake Nahuel Huapí. The inn overlooks a huge boca, where a sizable river empties into the lake. You can wade and fly-fish the boca—spinning is not allowed—or you can rent a boat and troll. I suggest you confine your boat fishing to the two hours prior to sunup; then, if you can afford it, another two hours in the evening. The inn's gardens, silhouetted against the broad expanse of the lake, are magnificent, and your wife will love them even if she doesn't fish. The flags of many countries are painted on the ceiling of the bar and dining room, and below each flag is the name of the fisherman from that country and the weight of his trophy fish. Only fish taken on flies count. When last I was there, there was no United States flag flying. Some American needs to get a 15-pound brown or rainbow and put the Stars and Stripes overhead.

Argentina is also down under, where the browns go up to 30 pounds and where the landlocked salmon world's record of 26 pounds and some ounces has been unofficially broken by Guy Dawson, a famous Argentine guide, who took a 34-pounder in the Traful's Pool of Plenty. Fish in Argentina run to record size, including both the brook trout and the rainbow.

In addition to Junín, you should fish the Bariloche area, both the Limay River and Lake Nahuel Huapí, with Laddie Buchanon. Every year brown trout of over 20 pounds are taken from both. For this fishing, contact Charles Boyd Buchanon, Las Heras 2948, 4 H, Buenos Aires, Argentina. Or if you write between December 1 to April 15, send your

This size rainbow can be caught in Argentina.

The inn at Correntoso, roughly a 50-mile bus trip from Bariloche, Argentina.

ROBERT WARNER

letter to him at Gutierrez 836, Bariloche, Rio Negro, Argentina. He is an excellent fisherman and splendid company.

Australia, Kenya, Lebanon, Iran, India's Kashmir, Japan, Chile, Brazil, Paraguay, England, Ireland, Scotland, Belgium—there are so many places where I have enjoyed excellent fishing, scenery, and company too, but space is limited.

In conclusion, what are the best ways to find out where the fishing you want is to be found, where to locate the best guides, or, if you are on a limited budget, where to camp out or stay in an inn and fish without a guide? What is the best time of year and what flies in what sizes should you take or buy? Read the outdoor magazines. Most of them carry one overseas story an issue. Write the author, tell him you enjoyed his piece, and give him a list of the questions you want to ask. Or, much better, go and see him. That's the way I met the late Joe Brooks. I traveled to Virginia to ask him about Argentina. He talked for three hours while I took notes. Since I have become an outdoor writer, I have done the same thing for many anglers who wanted to visit places that I have described. Authors are complimented by your interest, so don't be shy.

As conditions change, don't expect the author of a book or story written twenty years ago to give you up-to-date information. Confine your research to pieces published within the last year or two.

My son Jono with 11¼ pounds of brook trout taken in Quebec.

My Lebanese guide with one of our rainbows.

ROBERT WARNER

Or you can write the country's Director of Sport Fishing. In this way I was put in touch with Australia's Vic McCrystal, a top fishing writer, and together we enjoyed one of the best weeks of fishing I have ever had. For the Director's name, address, and proper title, contact the country's embassy in Washington, D.C.

Some years ago I asked a friend to fish with me for salmon in Scotland. He sent his deposit of several hundred dollars for fishing rights, and then he could not make the trip because he put off the business of getting a passport until the day before his departure. Of course, he couldn't get one on that short notice. Unless you have traveled overseas recently, read the rest of this chapter carefully.

Before applying for a passport, have a photograph taken and regulation-size prints made: two for your passport, another one for an International Driver's License, assuming you need one (the license can be obtained through the AAA), and a few extras just in case. I have had to give a photo to a customs official to get my rods through and, in another country, to get camera equipment in.

Apply at least four weeks ahead for a passport. Most federal buildings and city post offices issue them. Make sure you need one; in Canada and in some Central and South American countries a passport is not required. In Mexico all you need is a Tourist Identification Card with the limit of your stay dated. Be sure that the expiration date of your tourist card allows plenty of time for an unanticipated stay in that country. Unless you want to experience a Mexican jail—an adventure, I understand, one is better off without—don't overstay the expiration date no matter how wonderful the fishing.

When you apply for your passport, check to see if any visas are needed. Not all countries require them, but most African and Asian countries do. Getting these takes time, and you will have to apply by letter or call the nearest consulate.

If you need further information, write the U.S. Passport Office, 1425 K Street, N.W., Washington, D.C. 20524.

Go to your local doctor and ask him to give you the necessary shots, if any, for the country or countries you are heading for. Your doctor will give you the required International Health Certificate, properly filled out. He will also tell you where to go for a yellow fever shot, if this is required. Try to attend to this four weeks before departure in case you have a bad reaction from one of the shots or need to have two shots, such as those for cholera and typhoid.

On a fishing trip Murphy's Law can sit on your shoulder. A backup outfit can save the day if something happens to your favorite rod or reel.

Pack your rods carefully. A roll of masking tape is the answer. Lay your rods on the floor, and line them up so that the butt of at least one rod extends beyond the tips of the others on each side. Then tape the rods together. If a rod tip extends beyond the butt on either side, that tip will arrive broken. Clothing and raingear can be wrapped around the rods to help protect them and can be used to stuff empty spaces in the rod case.

And now a final warning (I write this with feeling, having once taken a pair of leaky waders to the subarctic, where I fished for a week in ice cold water in khaki pants): Test your waders before you go. Either wade a stream, or put them on and sit in a tub until you know whether or not they are watertight. And to be on the safe side, take a wader repair kit along.

My Favorite Places to Fish	*Type of Fish*	*Best Time*	*Suggested Flies* Type	Size
Papaskwasati River, Northern Quebec, Canada	Brook	September	1. Hairwing Coachman 2. White Wulff 3. Indispensable	8–14 8–14 8–14
Lake Wanaka, New Zealand	Rainbow Brown	February	1. Twilight Beauty 2. Nimmes Killer 3. Purple Grouse	12–14 12–14 12–14
Esquel, Argentina	Landlocked salmon	February	1. White Wulff 2. Hairwing Coachman	8–10 8–10
Lower Sindh, Kashmir, Northern India	Brown	September	1. Quill Gordon 2. Blue Bivisible 3. Black Gnat	20 20 20
Nuwarh—Eliya River, Ceylon, India	Rainbow	January	1. Black Bivisible 2. Light Cahill 3. Blue Bivisible	14–16 14–16 14–16

OTHER PLACES TO FISH OVERSEAS

In one chapter on overseas fishing, it is impossible to touch on the many places there are to dry-fly fish. In his chapter, Robert Warner has confined himself to giving the reader a taste of fishing in Norway, Quebec, New Zealand, and Argentina. For those readers who are interested in a brief report on a few of the other countries where there is excellent dry-fly fishing, below is a brief report. It is a consensus of several experts, but it is only as current as this book's publishing date. —J.M.M.

Australia (Tasmania)
Suggested Locations	New South Wales: Snowy, Thredbo, and Styx rivers; Eucumbene River and Lake Tasmania: Great Lake, Shannon, and South Esk rivers
Best Time	New South Wales: January, February, March Tasmania: September through mid-December
Local Contact	Vic McCrystal (fishing writer), Cardwell, Australia

Austria
Suggested Locations	Traun, Mur, Koppen Traun, and Lammer rivers
Best Time	July 15–August 15
Local Contact	Jon Springer's Erben (Tackle Shop), Graben 10, Vienna 1; Austria

British Columbia
Suggested Locations	Vancouver Island: Cowichan and Little Qualicum rivers Kamloops District: Adams River; Paul and Le Jeune lakes
Best Time	May and June
Local Contact	Echo Lodge, Kamloops, British Columbia, Canada

Chile
Suggested Locations	Liucura, Enco, Cautin, and Cumilahue rivers
Best Time	December 15–March 31
Local Contact	Adrian Dufflocq, Cumilahue, Llifen, Chile

England
Suggested Locations	Test, Itchen, Ribble, and Avon rivers
Best Time	May and June
Local Contact	Dermot Wilson, Nether Wallop, Hampshire, England

Ireland
  Suggested Locations   Robe River (County Mayo); Fergus River
                                      (County Clare); Corrib and Ennel Loughs
  Best Time   June, July and August
  Local Contact   Ashford Castle, Cong, County Mayo, Ireland

Sri Lanka (Ceylon)
  Suggested Locations   Nuwara Eliya, Adams Peak, and Horton's Peak
                                      rivers
  Best Time   March and April
  Local Contact   Ceylon Fishing Club, Nuwara Eliya, Ceylon

CHRISTINE FONG

Memo in Preparation for Fishing Trip

Duplicate this memo. Keep one copy in case of any problems, and leave the other copy at home.

Places where I will be staying:
  Name and Address:
  Dates: From: To: Contact:
                From: To: Contact:

Transportation:
  Destination   Airline   Tel.   Airport   Flight No.   Depart   Arrive

  Going:
  Return:

Entry Requirements:
  Passport   Visa   Vaccinations &   Foreign currency
                                      inoculations

Equipment Taken:
  Camera (name and serial number)   Rods, reels (name and description)
  Lens (name and serial number)
  Radio (name and serial number)
  Binoculars (name and description)

Credit Cards: Traveler's Checks:
  Company   Numbers
  Card number   Notify in
  Notify in case of loss   case of loss

Medical Info and Needs:
  Allergies   Blood type   Prescription medicines
  Antihistamines   Prescription eyeglasses
  Antibiotics   Physician's name, address, phone

  In case of emergency, notify:

Shopping for Family and Friends:
  Person's name   Shoe size   Dress size   Shirt size   Suit size   Other items

  _____

  _____

  _____

J. Michael Migel was born in New York, but his early years were spent in Arizona. He returned to New York to follow a career in finance.

He is a founding director of the American League of Anglers and was a member of the group that started the Bass Research Foundation. He belongs to the Angler's Club of New York, Theodore Gordon Fly-fishers, the Federated Fly Fishermen, and Trout Unlimited.

As a fisherman in the late 1920s, he helped popularize the Sea of Cortez as a saltwater angler's paradise and angled from Bimimi, Yucatán, and Mexico and in many other spots in the Atlantic and Pacific. In later years trout and salmon have become his deep loves.

His articles and short stories have appeared in numerous sports magazines, and he also edited The Stream Conservation Handbook.

17. The Future of the Dry Fly

J. Michael Migel

"DON'T MOVE," Len Wright whispered. "I've seen a fish flash, and I'm going to try him with a dry."

We'd been fishing the Miramichi, and near noon, noticing Len's rod tucked under his arm as he changed flies, I'd waded over to ask for his suggestions as to what fly I should use. Now I stood on his left.

"Quiet," he said, a sharp authority in his voice. "That fish won't touch a wet; maybe he'll come for a dry."

His rod bent and straightened until the length of line was right. Then the big, hairy White Wulff lit on the water and quickly bobbed its way downstream. Three times this happened. Then, on the fourth cast, one of the loveliest, most exciting dramas in all fishing unfolded.

The sun was at our backs, high enough so that the light penetrated rather than refracted from the water. The stones, boulders, and rubble underneath the four-foot, fast-moving cover were rounded shadows. From this underseas world,

> Where Alph, the sacred river, ran
> Through caverns measureless to man,

from these depths a form rose—slowly, deliberately—until it was only inches beneath its imitation prey, until in the perfect light its eye, the streamlining, the symmetry of its body, the silver blue-gray color, even perhaps the small black spots, were visible.

Temporarily forgotten was the reproductive urge; forgotten the evolutionary forces that sealed its gullet against food. Instead, for a moment or two, this exquisite salmon, in its memory, became again a parr, drifting back with the current to inspect an offering served in the surface film by its cradle, the river. Fanning its fins imperceptibly, glorying in its ability to navigate so expertly that it could maintain its exact position even when drifting backward in a sharp current, it floated downstream for two or three yards, constantly eyeing the bit of fluff and steel so short a distance above.

Then, as if Len hadn't been able to avoid drag and the fly skittered, or as if reality had given the fish a nudge and it thereupon recalled its rendezvous with destiny in some small brook upstream, like a mirage in a dream it sank to rest, hidden by the palisades and cavities of the floor below the current.

Twice more, like a wraith, it raised to inspect my companion's offering. Added to the engraved memory was the pulse-pounding excitement of "Would it take?" But like Greta Garbo, its final decision was "I vant to be alone."

The stream was the Westkill, which lives its life in the Catskills. Its beginnings, high in the wooded hills, are small: drops squeezed from brown humus, little runlets, and small trickles from springs whose guardian spirits are frogs reluctant to kerplunk when they are disturbed, probably because their house pools are too chilly.

This large brook rampages with the melt of snow and rises and falls with rainfall, but even in the dog days of July and August, several miles below its origins, the shrunken summer flow stays cool and fresh, bowered along most of its travels by trees and willows, foamed and bubbled by its twisting over, under, and about small and larger rocks. Most of the human inhabitants of this valley, and the summer visitors who vacation in the guest houses, treasure this lovely resource, but each year one or two more dwellings are built with new, bulldozed access roads, and more and more people picnic or camp heedlessly.

For at least a year, whenever I was in this part of the country, one pool in this stream was my classroom. In it lived a special trout. For a year this one fish gave me lessons in dry-fly fishing.

APRIL

Iron fraudators were hatching, and trout were gorging on their first spring feasting. Somehow I knew the rings in front of a deep undercut had to be made by a large fish. Overeager and careless, without studying the currents—trout this early in the season would be unsophisticated—I cast under the branches above where the circles had been quickly washed downstream. My Quill Gordon danced down the early spring race. In seconds it would be gulped, my rod would be raised, and a battle would be joined. A small vortex of roiled water eddied into the undercut, splitting with the main flow. My leader was snatched from its true path and my fly, like a puck on a hockey rink, skated.

In derision at such clumsiness, within inches of my dragging imitation, a big brown trout effortlessly seemed to climb out of the water, arched itself, splatted down, and then gracefully slid back underneath the hanging mass of small roots that shielded the undercut. My teacher had introduced himself.

On this late April day, on my first visit, the slot of a deer was still fresh enough to be leveling itself in the little patch of watery snow that still lingered underneath a giant shading hemlock, whose upper branches reached for the sky like the spire of a Gothic cathedral. On the bank close to the swollen stream, a few bared roots of this tree turned downward, curved as if they were the fingers of Antaeus himself, grasping the earth. Underneath them was a cave, the undercut chiseled by the eroding of flowing water and curtained by clumps of intertwined rootlets. This was the hold where my instructor lived.

MAY

My next lesson was during Hendrickson time. There was a new addition, a change on the surface of the pool. The bole of a large, dead maple tree had fallen to the ground. Slightly downstream from the undercut, its top lay halfway across the waters. Trapped by this partial dam were branches, beaver cuttings, leaves, and a bobbing empty beer can, all creating a miniature log jam.

In exactly the same spot where it had been three weeks earlier, near the cave but now also close to the flotsam, a good fish was feeding. On May 17 the waters were gentler and clear, so the sips were soft— "there was no slash, no swirl, just a light intake of water and another fly had disappeared." The dimples had to be made by my mentor.

Carefully backing away, I false cast on one side to avoid the low-hanging hemlock branches. My line lengthened. To be sure my leader and fly would clear the log jam, I deliberately overshot the target by four or five feet. The cast was good. There was curve and enough slack so when the currents floated my bribe in front of the undercut there wouldn't be any drag. Suddenly, quite a distance above the rise forms, where the big fish fed, there was a slash at my offering. My reflexes were too tight. I stuck. It was a 5-inch "brownie." I waited an hour, but the schoolmaster didn't resume his dining.

AUGUST

The day was hot, so I didn't study the pool until late afternoon. In this glen the mossy rocks pulsed a freshness, and scents were of green things, ferns, and wet earth. The silence was the aftermath of a still August day, a quiet so powerful that even the gurgling stream was muted.

Half an hour later, near the inlet, there was a splash—possibly the 5-incher. Then quickly, at two other stations, fish began to feed. At the proper time the elder statesman took his regular place at table.

Their supper was a small brownish-gray caddis. Unfortunately, the only flies in my boxes were mayfly imitations, so, unhappily, I knotted on a small Gray Fox Variant and later a size 16 Gray Fox, both proven takers on this stream. My sole reward was that my improved casts didn't put my tutor down. All my offerings were politely ignored, while the large brown continued gulping the stream's bounty, and once—to parade his self-confidence—he leaped clean out of his world to snatch a caddis that was hovering too close above him. Just before it turned too dark to be able to poke the nylon tippet through the eye of a fly, I tried a Cream Variant, but the fish's "Good night, class dismissed," was a tail slap, drowning my hopes.

SEPTEMBER

September 30 could have been a blue-sky day late in October. At the pool the voice of the wind talked through the heights of the trees. Sunlight, sieved through tossing leaves and swaying hemlock needles, shimmered and flickered on the partially shaded little flowing pond. A week earlier a quiet soaking rain had raised the level of the waters. This current must have pushed the platoon of drift and flotsam downstream from the dam of the half-floating dead maple snag, because now it lay on the water naked and almost alone. One tendril of a Virginia creeper, on a daring expedition to cross the pool, had crawled far out on this log. Its leaves, already a brilliant scarlet, trembled constantly from the vibrations of the wood as it temporarily held firm against the insistent shove of the current on its underbelly. In the wash, caught on a stub of a branch, swam a piece of white shredded plastic.

The current, lapping the tops of my boots, seemed warm as I first stood in my usual place twenty feet below this log, but during the ten-minute wait for the disturbance caused by my wading to quiet, it felt much chillier. Every once in a while a beam from the sun spotlighted a small shower of chickadees, early migrants that *dee-dee*'d from absurd

upside-down angles. There was little surface activity. It was too late in the year for mayflies or caddis to hatch in abundance, causing trout to slurp from stations, but my legs grew much warmer when I spied my instructor, prowling for any food carried by the lazy surface film, rise once not far from his usual lie.

Three times earlier during the year I'd hooked smaller trout in this pool. Because of my stance downstream from the log, playing even a small trout had presented many problems. Before I landed it, I'd had to keep the fish high in the water with rod pressure while I waded to shore and stumbled until I was above the obstruction. With those tactics, if the pool master even condescended to try my fly, the only possible results of hand-to-hand combat would be a broken 5X tippet wrapped around the roots deep in the undercut.

The late Joe Brooks once described taking a good trout in Maryland, which was rising upstream from him across a log. If I could remember the details in those paragraphs, didn't panic, and my prey dropped his guard, that reading offered a possible solution.

An ant tied on a No. 12 hook was the point of my weaponry. My first cast drew a blank. On the second, my imitation terrestrial, barely visible on the water, again floated over the exact spot I knew so well. An instinct betrayed the monster grown large and wise through caution and experience—an instinct to snatch at any food this late in the season that would add fat for his winter's semihibernation. He took like a barracuda.

Instantly, my hand raised the rod high. And, at the same time, I drove the butt hard at the fish. The split cane curved almost double under the vicious strain. The pressure on the bamboo, the leader, the hold of the hook in the fish's mouth was terrible, but it worked. Boosted by the speed of his own take and unable to head for the bottom, the big brown skidded over the water and across the top of the log. He was in my side of the pool.

Ten anxious minutes later surrender was inevitable. Like most big fish, his fight had been rushes, boring and angry terrier headshakes. Now, despite thrashings on the surface, he yielded to the incessant pressure, canted on one side, and finned in the shallows close to my feet. I reached with my net and put a slight extra strain on the bowed rod. It snapped upright. The line, leader, and ant flew past my head. It was incredible, unbelievable. For a long moment the shock was almost unsupportable. My opponent, my teacher, my friend just lay there. The red of his gills showed as the covers flared again and again. He righted himself with only his fins moving. Slowly at first, then steadily, he swam away. Like the flash of the sun from a mirror, he disappeared in the depths of his pool.

Trout fishing was over for the year, but ahead lay the winter in which to dream about the mistakes, the victories, the "what-might-have-beens." On cold nights I would sit before the fireplace and imagine the seasons in the misty future. Experience would tell me not to believe those golden fantasies, but the dreams would roll on. Days would never be bitter. There would be no weariness, no biting insects, and the fish— the fish would be huge, and I would master them well and truly. My dreams this winter would be of a wise brown, and his rise to my dry fly.

That night I recounted my adventure to my wife and to Lita and Art Flick, at whose home in the Catskills we are often privileged to visit. Then somewhat later, from the depths of an easy chair, I asked "The Laird of the Westkill" about his thoughts on the future of dry-fly fishing.

"When I first started fishing," Art answered thoughtfully, "a man using a dry fly was a curiosity, a nut. Today, after the early worming season is over, you'll find a great many men—especially older men— throwing a dry fly. As a breed, they are true sportsmen who welcome a challenge, who love the excitement of seeing a fish take on top. Many of them are becoming conservation-minded and find it easier to remove a dry from the mouth of a fish they intend to release.

"But what worries me is not the future of the dry fly—that's assured—but what about the future of all fishing? Each season more and more people come to the country, and there are more and more fishermen. But always there is the same amount of water. No, that's not right; there is less and less pure water each year. We shouldn't be talking about the future of the dry fly; we should talk about the future of fishable water."

My Favorite Places to Fish	Type of Fish	Best Time	Suggested Flies Type	Size
Schoharie Creek, Lexington, New York	Brown	May	1. Hendrickson	12–16
			2. Gray Fox	12–16
			3. Cream Variant	12–16
Batten Kill, Manchester, Vermont	Brown	Early June	1. Hendrickson	12–16
			2. Blue Wing Olive	16–18
			3. Cream Variant	14–16
Big Hole River, Montana	Rainbow Brown	September	1. Grasshopper	10–14
			2. Spiders	10–14
			3. Big Variants	10–14
Miramichi River, Doaktown, New Brunswick, Canada	Atlantic salmon	June	1. White Wulff	8–12
			2. Royal Coachman	8–12
			3. Alder Fly	8–12
Ausable River (both branches), Wilmington, New York	Brown Rainbow	Late June	1. March Brown	12–16
			2. Gray Fox Variant	12–16
			3. Rat-faced McDougal	12–16

List of Conservation Groups

DRY-FLY FISHERMEN have always been in the forefront of the fight for clean water and sensible conservation. Here is a selected list of conservation groups, public and private:

AMERICAN FISHERIES SOCIETY
1319 19th Street, N.W.
Washington, D.C. 20036

AMERICAN LEAGUE OF ANGLERS (ALA)
810 18th Street, N.W.
Washington, D.C. 20006

AMERICAN RIVERS CONSERVATION COUNCIL
324 C Street, S.E.
Washington, D.C. 20003

BASS
P.O. Box 3044
Montgomery, Alabama 36109

BROTHERHOOD OF THE JUNGLE COCK
10 East Fayette Street
Baltimore, Maryland 21202

BUREAU OF OUTDOOR RECREATION
United States Department of the Interior
Washington, D.C. 20240

BUREAU OF SPORT FISHERIES AND WILDLIFE
United States Department of the Interior
Washington, D.C. 20240

ENVIRONMENTAL DEFENSE FUND, INC.
162 Old Town Road
East Setauket, New York 11733

ENVIRONMENTAL PROTECTION AGENCY
United States Waterside Mall
Washington, D.C. 20460

FEDERATION OF FLY FISHERMEN (FFF)
15513 Haas Avenue
Gardena, California 90249

NATIONAL MARINE FISHERIES SERVICE
3300 Whitehaven Parkway
Washington, D.C. 20240

NATIONAL PARK SERVICE
U.S. Department of the Interior
Washington, D.C. 20250

NATURAL RESOURCES DEFENSE COUNCIL
1710 N Street, N.W.
Washington, D.C. 20036

RESTORATION OF ATLANTIC SALMON IN AMERICA, INC. (RASA)
Box 164
Hancock, New Hampshire 03449

SPORT FISHING INSTITUTE
Suite 801
608 13th Street, N.W.
Washington, D.C. 20005

STRIPED BASS FUND, INC.
45-21 Glenwood Street
Little Neck, New York 11362

THEODORE GORDON FLYFISHERS, INC. (TGF)
24 East 39th Street
New York, New York 10016

TROUT UNLIMITED (TU)
4260 East Evans Avenue
Denver, Colorado 80222

WATER POLLUTION CONTROL FEDERATION
3900 Wisconsin Avenue, N.W.
Washington, D.C. 20016

Note: A conservation directory, with a complete listing of prominent organizations and individuals engaged in conservation work, is available for $2.00 from THE NATIONAL WILDLIFE FEDERATION 1412 16th Street, N.W., Washington, D.C. 20036.